ANTHROPOLOGICAL PAPERS OF
THE UNIVERSITY OF ARIZONA

NUMBER 14

LYNNE
SCOGGINS
CRUMRINE

CEREMONIAL EXCHANGE AS A MECHANISM IN TRIBAL INTEGRATION AMONG THE MAYOS OF NORTHWEST MEXICO

THE UNIVERSITY OF ARIZONA PRESS

TUCSON 1969

ANTHROPOLOGICAL PAPERS OF
THE UNIVERSITY OF ARIZONA
NUMBER 14

LYNNE
SCOGGINS
CRUMRINE

CEREMONIAL EXCHANGE
AS A MECHANISM
IN TRIBAL INTEGRATION
AMONG THE MAYOS
OF NORTHWEST MEXICO

THE UNIVERSITY OF ARIZONA PRESS
TUCSON 1969

PREFACE

This study is the result of a year's field residence among the Mayo Indians of Sonora, Mexico, and several years' study in Yaqui and Mayo culture and society by my husband, N. Ross Crumrine, and me, in which there has been a constant interchange of ideas and information. From November 3, 1960, through December 15, 1961, Ross and I maintained residence in Mayo country, returning for two short periods from one to six weeks to Tucson. In addition to my husband's substantial contribution of work and thought to this dissertation, the positive effect of his confidence and dedication both during and after the fieldwork period is also acknowledged here. The generosity with which he has shared both work and creative energy has made possible the writing of this dissertation, as well as the field research.

The fieldwork and the writing on which this dissertation is based was financed under a Social Science Research Council Predoctoral Fellowship supplemented by a National Institutes of Mental Health Fellowship. Much of the writing was done during the tenure of a Wenner-Gren Predoctoral Research Grant. These financial sources have permitted a freedom in research for which I am truly grateful.

For personal, economic, and moral support above and beyond the call of duty in the form of special comfort to my family during research and writing, special mention is due to Norman R. Crumrine and Gertrude F. Scoggins.

Acknowledgments in the scholastic arena are more than deserved by each member of my dissertation committee. I am grateful to Dr. Malcolm McFee for many helpful suggestions in his reading of the final draft. Dr. Richard Woodbury, United States National Museum, Washington, D.C., on my committee at the inception of the work, provided particular encouragement to the development of thought at an early stage of field research and writing. To him I am indebted for infusions of courage at disheartening moments and for many insights, particularly into Southwestern Indian economy. Dr. Edward P. Dozier has given an understanding and appreciative reading, and it has been rewarding to have had the benefits of his critical understanding. To Dr. Harry T. Getty, I am grateful for interest, honest appraisal, the generous dedication of time, and extension of kindness both in the early stages and later, as deadlines approached. To the director of the dissertation, Dr. Edward H. Spicer, I want to give special credit for sharing his penetrating understanding of both the data and the theory involved, for it has been developed in large part as a dialogue with him. I join so many of those students who have worked with him in appreciation for the time, talent, and human concern he finds for students and colleagues. Also I wish to thank Dr. William C. Lawton of California State College at Hayward for helpful suggestions concerning the final draft of the manuscript. Though their scholastic discipline has at times seemed severe, I am grateful to all these people for the degree of maturity this process of rethinking may have brought about in my anthropological training.

To the people of those Mayo communities in Sonora and Sinaloa with whose social organization this dissertation is concerned, I offer heartfelt thanks for hospitality, at times tolerance, and frequently faith and generously given insights into social life and symbolism. I defer to Mayo custom in not singling out particular individuals for public acknowledgment, though their names are well known in the pueblos where they serve with dedication in offices and sodalities. Offered not in place of friendship, but with it, like a promise being fulfilled, this is the continuation of an effort to demonstrate to others part of the esthetic complexity and essential intelligence of design for survival in the Cahitan way of life, in religion, language, political, and economic institutions.

CONTENTS

ILLUSTRATIONS

ABSTRACT

The social organization of the Mayos of Northwest Mexico is characterized by a number of social units complexly related to one another. The most important of these are a native variety of Catholic church, saints' cults, a large number of sodalities whose membership does not seem to be ascribed by kinship in any highly fixed way, loosely structured residence groups combined with bilateral kinship organization, and ritual kinship. Authority and command structures within the pueblo church unit are specialized as to type of authority (judicial, religious, economic, and so on). In addition, some authority relationships are hierarchical, as within sodalities, and some imply only the authority to coordinate other groups, or to put pressure on essentially autonomous though complementary groups to cooperate.

Between Mayo churches and households a variety of exchange relationships prevail. These are illustrated with particular emphasis on the patron saint exchange system. An analysis of this exchange system demonstrates that, while internal integration of each pueblo unit is organic, intercommunity exchange between pueblo churches in the patron saint exchange system is dominantly mechanical or the combination of like units. The entire list of officials and sodalities from one community joins another, sodality for sodality, rank for rank, within the sodality.

Food distribution is an important correlate of intercommunity ceremonial exchange among Mayos. This economic ethic is associated with all Mayo ceremonial activity and helps distinguish Mayos from non-Mayos. Mestizo churches do not take part in reciprocal feasting or in the other intricate ritual and mythical patterns diagnostic of ceremonial exchange. The concept of ceremonial exchange thus provides a tool for drawing ethnic boundaries.

Furthermore, ceremonial exchange is patterned in such a way as to group pueblos in paired and opposing relationships at increasingly higher levels. These relationships correspond in fairly high degree to the geographical distance and recency of fission between the groups involved. The same type of massing, then, can be shown to exist among Mayos in one sense as in Tiv or Nuer society, for example. But it is important to note that while massing is based among these African tribes upon lineage structure, or small kinship descent groups, the parallel kind of massing among Mayos appears to be dominantly based upon local cult segmentation, which is not strictly determined by kinship or residence, while it is definitely though loosely influenced by both these in a variety of ways.

Rituals confirming segmentary sociability at different levels of massing are briefly described.

The level of development of Mayo social organization through each historical period is then described from historical data with reference to population changes, changes in economic organization and land-holding systems, levels of social organization of enemy groups, situations of war or peace and methods of conducting war and negotiating or maintaining peace, native leadership and religious cults or churches throughout the periods. The approximate period and cultural ecology in association with which each feature of the present organization originated is suggested.

The type of social integration characterizing Mayo society today is perhaps dominantly tribal because of the lack of strictly hereditary offices and the central importance of pan-tribal sodalities, yet many characteristics of the organization reflect chiefdom-like features, and even features of state organization. Presently the population explosion, interethnic pressures, and increasing tightness of land boundaries and available land promise to require real breakthroughs in Mayo social development, which has been characterized by intense magical nativism for the last seventy or eighty years.

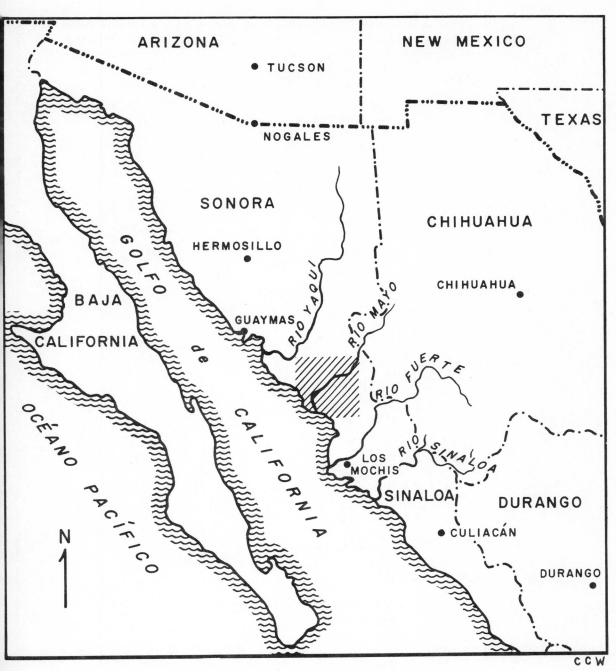

Map 1. Northwest Mexico. (From Crumrine, N.R.,
The House Cross of the Mayo Indians of Sonora, Mexico)

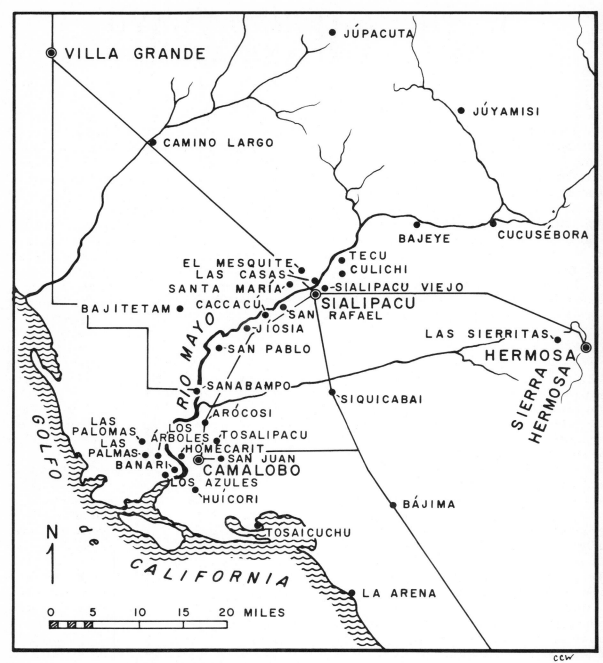

Map 2. Some Mayo River Valley Pueblos. (From Crumrine, N.R.,
The House Cross of the Mayo Indians of Sonora, Mexico)

1. THE NATURE OF MAYO SOCIAL ORGANIZATION

INTRODUCTION

The Mayo Indians who occupy the lower valley of the Mayo River of Sonora, Mexico, live in scores of scattered *rancherías* or clusters of several related households, in forty or fifty small pueblos of one hundred to several hundred people, and in *barrios*, or districts, around and in the four larger Mexican towns of the area. They live to a large degree interspersed with mestizos and non-Mayos in almost all communities. However some communities tend to be far more homogeneous than do others. Most Mayo communities claim at least ten to twenty percent non-Mayo residents, and many are more than half non-Mayo in their ethnic identification. In many Mayo households and churches, the Mayo language, of Uto-Aztecan affiliation, is still spoken.

From the northeast to the southwest the course of that part of the Mayo River area which is inhabited by these people runs through three ecological zones. Sandy coastline with salt deposits yields fish, shells, salt, and other ocean products. Less than a mile or two inland in some areas the palms and mangroves of the saline swamp area give way to a thick growth of giant pitaya and smaller varieties of cactuses. This area provides building materials and a wide variety of medicines and natural fruits and seeds. Further inland a third zone characterized by mesquite, cactuses, and agaves begins at slightly higher elevations. Numerous harder woods and forest products abound here. Fertile soils characterize the river region and are exploited agriculturally by Mayos as well as by the non-Mayo residents of the region.

Traditionally the main Mayo crop was corn supplemented by beans and squash. Today cotton, wheat, sesame, and other oil grains are also grown by Mayos. In addition, the harvesting of truck farm vegetables such as tomatoes, peas, chiles, and some fruits such as oranges, grown by large-scale non-Mayo farmers in the area, provides a source of wage labor to Mayos. Fishing, both in cooperatives and by kin units is important for cash and subsistence. Wage labor on farms is probably the largest single source of cash income to Mayo families, though many families farm and market their own crops. They farm both on small plots and in *ejidos*, communal land-holding units which are obliged to maintain a close relationship with a federal financing system.

Thus, as far as residence and production aspects of the economy go, Mayos in this area are integrated into the state and national systems.

Yet, paradoxically, Mayo social organization continues to reflect a distinctive character apart from the mestizo social, economic, and political systems that surround it. This organization illustrates and typifies an interesting and theoretically significant level of sociocultural development. It is based primarily on the mechanism of ceremonial exchange, but it is also strikingly similar in some characteristics to segmentary lineage systems found in other parts of the world. In still other features it contrasts as a type with segmentary lineage systems, for it is not primarily or closely kin-based, certainly not on a unilineal type of kinship, and it differs in regard to the natural and human environmental matrices with which the appearance and persistence of segmentary systems are claimed to be associated.

Part of the significance of delineating this type of organization is in the idea that something resembling it would seem to characterize large numbers of societies in Latin America. In addition it has some definite resemblances to patterns of organization in other parts of the world, specifically in the Pacific and Southeast Asia areas (Leach 1954).

Barnes (1962), while apparently responding to the stimulating effects of the development and refinement of a segmentary lineage model for describing processes going on in some African societies (Evans-Pritchard 1940, Bohannon and Bohannon 1953, P. Bohannon 1958), finds this model unsuitable for Highland New Guinea tribes. He notes some of the following characteristics of some New Guinea groups: relative looseness of status determination by kinship descent, the pattern of multiple allegiance or shifting affiliation in local group membership, vagueness in tracing exact relationship between agnates, absence of activities bringing the agnatic core together as a unity, absence of an agnatic ancestor cult and apparently the indeterminate affiliation of women with natal or affinal groups. Together with these characteristics he proposes the need for a different concept of segmentation for a New Guinea model, one not based on the dogma of descent. He suggests no particular social mechanism or ideology (dogma), however, saying that this segmentation appears to be relatively arbitrary, as contrasted with lineage segmentation.

The significance of this observation is considerable. The recognition that the African model for analysis of social organization is no more appropriate for the Mayo materials than for the New Guinea, and that the reasons for this are similar, leads to the search for a new type of mechanism and ideology for segmentation.

There has also been an explicit recognition early in the literature on segmentary organization (Fortes 1936) that ceremonial exchange is an important mechanism of integration between groups. It often has important functions in kinship-descent-oriented societies as well as among those not using descent as the exclusive or even primary means of determining religious or local group memberships. In many parts of the world we find isolated villages maintaining links with one another and with adult members not currently resident in the villages, through the mechanism of ceremonial activities. Such patterns characterize present-day villages in the Philippines (Sibley 1960: 508) and in Mexican Indian villages (Bunzel 1952: 71-2, 84-5; Redfield and Villa Rojas 1934: 153; Lewis 1963: 44-5). These patterns, especially in Mexico and Guatemala, appear to be based on fusions of Catholic with aboriginal systems. They are not limited, however, to that context.

Both the generality of a similar pattern and the expectation that a concrete American Indian model can be formulated, at least limited to a cultural region within that area, lend this task significance for a theory of cultural evolution. Service (1962) has already noted that some tribes do not have a social organization based on lineal distinctions and that certain features of contact history or "superorganic environment" coincide with this difference.

It may be objected that the terminology applied here has been developed in cultural evolutionary theory for societies not known to have been in extensive firsthand contact with Western societies. Mayo society, on the other hand, has been in contact with some form of European-derived society for almost four centuries. In order to justify this, let us assume that contact with Western types of society is fundamentally analyzable in terms similar to those used in the analysis of contact with any other society or type of society. Though it may have stimulated the most fundamental changes in Mayo social organization to have come into contact with Spanish groups, and later with mestizo groups, Mayo social organization has continued nevertheless to evolve in a distinctive and patterned way separately from the local version of the intrusive mestizo society. The changes in each period of Mayo history up to 1890 are such that they can be analyzed just as if the intrusive society were another indigenous group rather than a modified form of Western derived society.

HYPOTHESIS

In its most fundamental characteristics Mayo internal organization seems to illustrate the concept of composite tribe as outlined by Elman Service (1962) in his recent book, *Primitive Social Organization, An Evolutionary Perspective*. Mayo social structure is characterized by a bilateral kinship system with what at first appear to be loosely structured residence groups and a wide variety of sodalities. Some of these sodalities are of the type that Service terms pantribal. Their structure is practically the same from one local community to another, and at times the membership of one community combines with that of another. Each community has a council, formed largely of sodality heads, much like that of any other Mayo community. Community councils combine on an intercommunity level in wider undertakings in a sort of mechanical integration. That is, they convene together with apparently equal voice in the activities at hand. Occasionally an unusually wide integration of communities occurs under charismatic leadership, the power of which may be re-enforced by approval from each community council. It appears to be within this kind of organization that Mayos have in recent times reached their widest extent of social integration or greatest complexity of development in social organizations.

Nevertheless, the type of integration which Service, after Durkheim, calls mechanical, the combination of like parts, appears at least superficially to be the dominant type of integration on the intercommunity level. We will, however, examine this idea more fully at a later point.

Sodalities that are now thought of as military societies, or that have now become exclusively ceremonial groups but in the past appear to have arisen from prehispanic warrior sodalities, form some of the most important pan-tribal sodalities among Mayos. A complex chain of ceremonial exchanges involving a number and variety of these sodalities forms a primary mechanism in a net of Mayo integration, up to what might be called a tribal level.

Now should we suggest the definite hypothesis that the essential nature of Mayo social integration is today tribal, even though it has long been a society in contact with Western society in one form or another, some assumptions are required. We have to assume that the present form of integration is related not only to the changes that have taken place in the physical environment and man's relation with it but also to changes in the human ecology — more finely said, a variety of significant aspects of the human environment, including conditions of contact.

Sahlins (1961) has suggested that the segmentary lineage systems of Africa, specifically those of the Tiv and Nuer, are a means of intrusion into an area or ecological niche which other groups are already exploiting, and that the system characterizes societies of the tribal level of development who are successful in competition and open conflict with other societies of the tribal level, not necessarily with groups of levels other than tribal. Evans-Pritchard suggested that the Nuer began to develop a chiefdom with the stimulus of Western contact until external forces (Western interference) stifled the leadership. Thus we have the recognition that (1) the level of social organization of surrounding groups and (2) the state of competition, or conflict with those groups, are two factors coinciding with the development of a segmentary lineage tribal level of social organization on the part of a group. Describing native prehispanic political systems of the Southwest United States, Spicer (1962: 378) points this out clearly.

Where tribal feeling was strongest and widest in scope — among the Mayos, Yaquis, and river Yumans — warfare was of fairly frequent occurrence at the time of the coming of the Spaniards. Warfare was by no means unknown to the Opatas, Pimas, and Tarahumaras, but there was less in the way of formal organization for fighting, and it appears to have been less of a focus of cultural interest. Probably the institutionalization of warfare had something to do with the different intensities of tribal feeling which existed.

Also, however, it is apparent that during times of peace drastic changes may occur in social organizations as responses to environmental changes emanating from human agents. The mission period for the Mayos, at least in the first seventy years, was characterized by rather highly structured cooperation rather than competition between the Spanish mission systems and the Mayo system. Mayo leadership and the older and influential people appear to have been receptive to the missionaries and the programs. Through borrowing and fusion, this receptivity resulted in changes, mostly additions, to Mayo technology and to foundations for later and farther reaching organizational and cultural changes. The changes originated in a peacetime intercultural environment that was cooperative rather than competitive. They were significant changes, and though at the time they did not basically alter the level of evolutionary development characterizing Mayo society, they did help make possible some later adaptations which brought the social complexity to a late tribal level probably far more cohesive in organization and distributional efficiency than the prehispanic organization, and able to hold its own against a frontier state for almost a hundred years.

It will become apparent in the following chapters that ceremonial integration is regarded as the key in understanding the nature of total Mayo social organization. The mutual transmutability of sodality-based military integrations into sodality-based ceremonial integrations, the heart of the system, is expressed by Edward Spicer (1945) in a discussion of Yaqui militarism. In striving to reconcile the warlike history of the Yaquis and Mayos with the essential Apollonian character of their social and cultural organization, Spicer focuses on the ceremonialization of the men's war sodalities and "ritualization of the aboriginal war interest" during the Jesuit period of Yaqui history, and he finds that "the strength of the Yaquis lay in the highly integrated church, civil, and military organization that lay rooted in the cultural renaissance of the Jesuit period." He sums up by proposing a basic similarity in sociocultural organization among several Southwest American Indian groups.

. . . The essential genius of the Yaquis, as fostered in their Pueblolike ceremonial and social organization, has been Apollonian, and that genius, strangely enough, they have expressed in war and conflict as consistently as the Pueblos have expressed in peaceful ceremony their similar genius (Spicer 1945: 48).

The contact conditions for Mayos were somewhat different from those for Yaquis in minor details, but the same basic historically formed culture and social organization characterizes both. And similar to the Yaqui social organization, the Mayo, in the decades since its military pacification, has emerged again, expressing its organizational genius in ceremonialism, but with ceremonial forms forged in long periods of conflict and tempered in periods of peaceful and vigorous cooperation, periods of renaissance.

With these kinds of ideas in mind, the hypothesis may be introduced, that the level of integration of Mayo social organization fits, with some variations, the ideal type which Service terms tribal. Its diagnostic traits are the presence of pan-tribal sodalities or institutions; religious, political, and economic autonomy of primary segments; and mechanical solidarity among tribal segments. Incipiently, its new organization arises out of the traditional one in partial response to natural environment and the presence of competing societies or superorganic features; but, becoming well integrated, it may persist longer than the environment in response to which it arose.

A great many societies are proliferations of the tribal ideal type: some small and some large, some lineal and some composite or cognatic in descent reckoning patterns (Service 1962: 110-42). All, however, are familistic, egalitarian, and lack separated bodies of political control, true economic specialization, and full-time religious professionalization. They are segmental, and each segment has much autonomy, which is a diagnostic feature, and one we will recognize in the following material, as the evidence for this pattern emerges repeatedly in Mayo society. The characteristic form of integration is, after all, the most important criterion of level of evolutionary development.

BASIC ECONOMIC STRUCTURES OF MAYO SOCIETY

Mayo technology is today characterized by wooden hoes and digging sticks beside tractors and combines; fences constructed of wild growth beside those of barbed wire; dugout log canoes beside fiberglass motorboats; machine-woven bedding beside blankets woven on a crude native loom. Wild fruits, unrefined ocean salt, fish and wild game still supplement food raised and purchased. Other earlier level technological items, such as native cane-and-mud and mat houses and unfired adobe houses, all with wooden corner-post construction, have little competition from more recent technological innovations such as fired adobe structures with floors and glass windows. This is perhaps largely due to the expense of these alternative materials and the scarcity of cash as compared with the ease of obtaining those dwellings which are made from the products that may be taken directly from the earth and its growth.

Bows and poisoned arrows and cane spears, used by hundreds of Mayo revolutionaries as late as 1915, would have been supplanted much sooner by guns, according to some of the veterans, but for the plain lack of availability of the guns and ammunition. Today mock rifles are the insignia of some ceremonial officials who formerly carried bows and arrows.

Other officials, less closely associated with literal, as against symbolic offense-defense, still carry lances.

Mayos really do not seem to have any mysterious or irresistible impulse to reject technological advantages they understand, and they are rather quick to comprehend the advantages of many technological tools and processes — such as tile drainage in saline soils, for example — which are not available to them for complex social, political, and economic reasons. They use what political power they have and can muster to get piped and pure water and electricity to their communities, and for large irrigation and drainage ditches. They struggle for many kinds of economic improvements. They have resisted opening lines of communication into their lands only insofar as those lines seemed to open them individually and collectively to exploitation — a point of view that can hardly be called backward. They have united and hired lawyers at times in the past to defend their property rights, sometimes with little success. With the failure at times of some of the technological and legal innovations and borrowings to serve their aims as envisioned, Mayos keep adapting to present circumstances upon the base of proved skills and social systems, though earlier Mayo forms have also become subtly changed in response to the pervasive environmental and dominantly contact produced transformations.

Skills and social organizations that were part of an earlier adjustment persist. Traces of an originally tripartite production system — hunting-gathering, agricultural, and fishing — persist, together with a fiesta distribution system. The social units of production, that is the groups which actually labor together, are still largely kin-based, even within the ejido, which is usually either dominantly Mayo in ethnic composition or dominantly non-Mayo, in the Mayo River area. It is in financing of crops and operation costs that Mayo economy is most closely tied to the dominant society today, and it is a relationship in which resides much power for institutions in the dominant society.

Many Mayo craft specialties persist, such as weaving cane and palm mats, and making fireworks and alcoholic drinks. Other crafts, such as pottery-making and basket-making, have all but vanished, being eliminated by availability of purchased ironware, tin cups, and, for fiesta cookery, galvanized tin washtubs. When certain types of handmade pottery are required — for baptism, confirmation of *mandas*, water jars — they are bought in the market. Some Mayo craft specialties are sold through the market in turn. Almost all Mayos know how to make and farm with traditional wooden digging sticks and pitchforks, cooperating in family and community-based production units in their own ejido plots and private lands. But many also know how to drive and care for complex large machinery, not only for wage work with large non-Mayo landowners but also in their own collective ejidos.

The main production units are still the household residence units and the local community, or, more accurately speaking, the sex-based work units that form within these units. Men form work groups with brothers-in-law, nephews, and resident kin males. Women form work groups with daughters, sisters-in-law, and females resident in the ranchería. Ejido assignments made to individuals in ejidos where those individuals have no resident kin cannot therefore be readily exploited by individuals, especially where heavy work like clearing large stands of thorn forest is involved.

The crops produced are often controlled through the bank-financing system rather than by personal choice of Mayo farmers — thus, for example, oil grains, cotton, and wheat, rather than corn, are common crops. This also relates, however, to the high saline content of the soil in most lower river lands, for which certain crops are more appropriate, as well as to demands of a national economy. Products are often sold commercially rather than distributed directly — even craft products having nothing to do with ejido financing systems. This is true in fishing and cattle-raising villages as well as in farming villages.

The increasing integration of Mayos into the Mexican market economy as a result of widespread changes in production and marketing and land tenure and management, and to some extent in the social organization of production — as in ejido-bank financing arrangements — has also indirectly affected the fiesta distribution system, though Mayos have not been caught up in an intense orientation toward the same type of buying and ownership that characterizes the local mestizos of the towns (Erasmus 1961: 209-37). In the Mayo fiesta system, on the other hand, money is used to buy items that were formerly from primary resources — food raised in one's own fields. But the use of money as such does not fundamentally change the fiesta economy into a market economy. As will become clearer in the course of discussion, its diagnostic feature is a ritual situation and rationale.

Clearly, the type of sociocultural integration characterizing Mayo society took its particular form before 1890, in the economic context of a predominantly agricultural economy in which hunting, fishing, and gathering of wild plant products for food, housing, and some kinds of clothing were important activities for obtaining supplementary resources. This economic pattern of production persists today together with the fiesta distribution system, though modified, in almost every Mayo household and community, supplemented with wages brought in from labor in the dominant society. It is combined with ejido organization which was originally designed to strengthen the local community and build it into the national life.

We can then see a combination of economic structures overlaying one another — one level in which local communities have an autonomous economic character, and another overlay in which primarily individuals rather than social units are in a fluctuating wage employment and spending relationship with members and institutions of the dominant society.

SOCIAL STRUCTURES INVOLVED IN CEREMONIAL EXCHANGE

Basic Social Structures

The basic social structures of Mayo life are pueblo, which as we shall see is not exclusively a residential unit among Mayos today; church; household; ranchería and other residence groups; kinship and ritual kinship groups; clientele groups and a variety of sodalities. Some of these overlap partially. In essence, church, ritual kin, and clientele groups serve as sodalities crosscutting other sodalities. For example clientele groups are customarily knit together by kin and ritual kin ties. But kin and ritual kin ties occur separately from clientele groups also, so that the additional concepts are required. A brief description of basic Mayo social structures is essential to this analysis. Mexican units, such as ejido and municipal and state organizations in which Mayos participate as individuals, will not be discussed here, as they are not directly involved in ceremonial exchange.

Pueblo

The pueblo is a small group of rancherías or clusters of related households with a historical tradition of having been one people, headed by a common council of officials closely associated with and incorporating a modified form of native Catholic church. A group of elders, or persons who have had long experience in positions of community responsibility, preside over the council in jural affairs. The power of this group today in some pueblos is less than the power residing in the heads of the church sodalities, though all power of council officials arises from approval of pueblo household heads and is felt to be a manifestation of supernatural permission.

People maintaining residence in a wide variety of rancherías, villages, and towns claim to belong to the pueblo where their church is located. Ultimately, the identification rests on an ancestor cult, an incisive common belief that they inherited the land on which the traditional graves are located. Even where dispersal and resettlement have taken individuals far from ancestral pueblos, they maintain in many instances the identification with the ancestral pueblo and belong to its church organization, traveling many miles to return and participate in its activities. After they have buried close relatives in two or more pueblos where they have maintained residence at one time or another, they may maintain allegiance to all or to any one pueblo.

Kinship and Residence

The household is an "amorphous" or composite group among Mayos today. Almost any kind of relative may be found in a given household. It is common to have married children of either parent living near the central household of the parents in small one-room structures without kitchens — all the family eating together at the larger dwelling. Parents' siblings and children, as well as more distant relatives, may be incorporated into the household, and household composition may change throughout the year for economic reasons.

Groups of households recognizing common kin ties and located together geographically form a ranchería or *barrio*. A group of these in turn — together with a group of officials and a council organization — constitutes a pueblo. A pueblo considered as a residential unit rather than an association then would be constructed in large part of simple kin units, were it not for the loose structuring of the root unit, the household. The bilateral kinship system has apparently allowed great latitude in residence patterns for some time. Many behavior patterns persist which were associated with a terminology or terminologies spottily known and not in wide use at the present time by Mayos except within the area of the nuclear family, where the Mayo terms are used vocatively and in reference in almost every household. Otherwise, Spanish terms have replaced the Mayo ones largely in a pattern that reflects a transitional or changing system (as in Pascua, Spicer 1940: 65, Figure 7).

The main outlines of the Mayo-Yaqui terminological system can be clearly reconstructed. It resembles in over-all form the Papago system as summarized by Rosamond Spicer (1949: 46) differing in some details.

In terms of roles the behavioral significance of the older-younger dichotomy reflected in the terminology lies in the nepotic relationship. A variety of specialized aunt and uncle roles which appear to have once characterized Mayo kinship are today weakening, though still taking enough form to make possible reconstruction. Uncles and aunts, in both maternal and paternal line, had special ritual, jural, and surrogate parent roles with respect to both nieces and nephews. Cousins were, moreover, classified through the relative age relationship of their parents to one's own connecting relative or parent.

The existence of terms for great-grandparents and great-great-grandparents and the extension of kinship to grandparents' siblings in both lines, according to informants, confirms the importance of maintaining a collateral as well as lineal account of relationship even two generations removed from the ego's. In terms of role this reflects the closeness of sibling groupings throughout life. Sibling relationships are characterized by cooperation and mutual aid and responsibility, especially as regards children.

Maternal and paternal roles stress protection and love in early childhood, and later both assume authority. Paternal roles particularly assume differentiation with regard to the sex of the child. Fathers and daughters have a respect relationship with some degree of avoidance, whereas fathers and sons work and perform ceremonial activities together. Closeness of parents in terms of affection and residential arrangements does not diminish with age. An old person with living children is assured of a home, and he may go from one to another of the households of his children at different seasons; or the children may come to live with parents at any time. Collaterals of grandparents and parents are treated similarly.

Grandchildren are ears for the tales and myths of the old ones. While the younger men and women labor in the fields and kitchens, the children play in the ramadas under the voices of grandmothers and grandfathers.

Marriage roles are characterized by mutual deference while partners retain self-possession and dignity and spend very little of their days together. The oldest woman in the household heads the women's work group and considers herself the head of the household until her husband comes home. At that time he becomes head of the household. He is, in turn, head of the men's work group in the absence of an older able man in the household. Formerly families of men and women played fixed and complex roles in mate selection and in the wedding ceremony (Beals 1943: 53, and similar to that described for Yaquis by Spicer 1940: 73-6). Many people do not go through the formal Mayo marriage ceremony today, although everyone agrees this is a serious omission of necessary ritual which will result in difficulties in the ceremonial status of the individual. Most people of middle age have had several spouses.

The ideal pattern of land inheritance is one of equal inheritance between children, older, younger, men and women alike. In case of actual request for division, this is what is usually recommended by a paternal uncle. But the preferred or perhaps prescribed pattern is that heirs continue to live together, work together, and pool the fruits of the inheritance in one household. Any women, or men, leaving the household would ask only for a share in the proceeds of the household if they share in its labor and bring resources to it. If they leave permanently they forfeit their rights. As women often marry out of the household, as the pattern works out, inheritance would appear to favor men. But test cases show that women also inherit and may bring husbands in to live on their land. Both men and women also own and inherit movable property, from cows to cooking vessels.

This system again shows the importance of residence over kinship relationship as such. If a person marries someone with land, he, or more usually she, does not need to claim land from parents or siblings. Unused lands formerly reverted to a common fund of village lands, used by everyone for gathering wood, fruits, and medicines.

Outside the ejido system, and before its inception, at the pueblo level as well as at the household level, the whole group owned the land. Those who forsook the close residence unit lost their rights, whether men or women. They might later return and take up their inheritance, however. The ideology of inheritance is that all inherit equally so long and only so long as they are in the household and form part of its work groups. Consequently every household and pueblo strives to keep as many resident members as it can, which gives it a right to more land and makes it a prosperous and strong group. Its members guard its solidarity and dozens of Mayo phrases express the ideal that it should not be divided within itself. Some non-ejido land is today deeded to individuals, but land-use patterns still adjust to the customary pattern described above.

Most Mayo households are indeed extended in some way. The occasional family which appears to be neolocal has a lineal or collateral kinsman living in the household at some time in the year.

The patterns illustrated by residence groups are certainly not consistently lineal. A household attempts to attract to itself male as well as female affines. The loss of a member is a loss of power and may entail land loss through the inability to use it. An older couple strive to teach their children value for remaining with their inheritance, which has religious meaning as well as, perhaps more than, economic meaning.

The ideology of the household appears to have been applied in a somewhat literal way to the church. "Our church has many children (ʾasoaka)" is a way of saying that it is a very good church, just as a family is good because it is big in terms of numbers of people. Nothing more scathing, on the other hand, could be said of another pueblo than that "they don't have many people." It is to imply perhaps that they are losing out in the competition for essentials — people first of all, the workers; land and wealth secondarily, for these relate to health of the people. No lineal principle limits the composition of residence units. The pressures members may use to acquire affines are normally exercised through the marriage of women, though there is some evidence that arranged marriages are pretty much a thing of the past. The sororate and levirate would have once helped to consolidate potential younger sibling-older sibling divisions. Some economic and residence behavioral patterns ordinarily associated with these arrangements persist. With the Christian ethical system, polygyny has lapsed. In contradiction, however, a man who is able to support more than one woman would be thought selfish not to do so, while he is, at least overtly, denied the sexual privileges formerly allowed to him in return.

The terminology associated with this kinship system is no longer in everyday use except within the nuclear family, where it is prescribed in most Mayo families. Kinship is declining as a regulating feature of social life because it no longer regulates marriage to the extent that it did before, the men of the household being less able to enforce their privileges and duties along this line than before, and because of the fact that ejido farm lands could not be inherited. Ejido-associated land patterns have also contributed to the pattern of couples living together without being married, some informants suggest. The weakening of the kinship system is connected with changes in ethical systems as well as economic systems, rapid depopulation and dislocation of families in long periods of war, all of which have taken place at different periods throughout the last four centuries. Considering the length of Spanish and Mexican contact and the concomitant environmental changes, we are actually pressed to explain the persistence of those traces of a distinctively Mayo kinship pattern which do persist.

The main function of kinship in the total web of Mayo life today is the economic interdependence of resident relatives; the maintenance of the ancestor cult; and the regulation of marriage, exogamic with respect to household and ranchería as well as the known bilateral kin group. However, as we will point out, kinship alone does not regulate the ancestor cult, for example. And in marriage regulation the residential kin unit shares with the non-kin residence unit, the pueblo, for some informants claim that pueblo membership once had regulatory functions with regard to marriage.

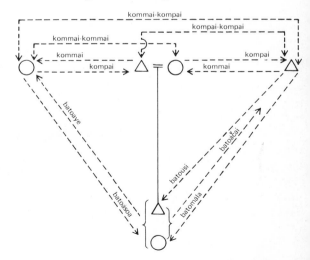

Figure 1. Mayo ritual kinship terms of reference. (Diagram adapted from Spicer, 1940, Fig. 8.)

The kinship system shares all its functions except the most primary — those relating to the nuclear family — with the ritual kinship system (Figure 1). The terms applied to ritual kin are most frequently Mayo, though Spanish equivalents are sometimes used. Ritual kin, in addition to important ceremonial functions — the diagnostic element of this relationship — are also occasionally taken into households in the same pattern as actual kin. Kin and ritual kin statuses may overlap. Ritual kin provide a mutual aid circle similar to the kin group of an individual, both economically and socially. Nets of ritual kinship bind together clientele groups of curers and re-enforce the political power of high officials and sodality heads. In general, ritual kinship as an integrative element in Mayo social organization at least equals kinship in importance, and perhaps exceeds it because of the internal integration which it effects in clientele and sodality groups and across pueblo and other division lines. Kinship also results in similar patterns of integration, but with less pervading and consistent thoroughness because of the fact that the nets of strong diadic and small group relationships which can form within real kinship are restricted by necessity of prior consanguineous or genetic ties. Ritual kinship is limited by no such conditions and is thus a rather interesting form of tribe-wide sodality, which runs like a latticework through the social structure re-enforcing other sodalities within themselves and tying them together.

Sodality

Most central to the discussion of Mayo social integrative devices is the type of social unit we term sodality. These units are very significant from the Mayo point of view. Mayo society values the individual in terms of his sodality memberships and participation record. A list of each Mayo's ancestors — but only the distinguished ones — is kept in a small book and prayed over in household and cemetery rituals throughout the year from time to time. In this book the individual dead are listed according to name, date of death, and sodality participation. The ritual and type of funeral due a person relates specifically to the sodalities he has belonged to and participated in during his lifetime.

Rather than asking a man's name to locate him in a town or community, it is much more successful to ask for him by his sodality status and rank within that sodality. Mayos identify one another by

sodality and length of service and responsibility of participation in the sodalities, rather than by kin status on the whole. This is in strong contrast to the Hopis, for example, another Southwestern society strongly kin-based in social organization. While kinship as an organizing principle in Mayo life appears to be losing some of its clarity and importance, sodalities have become an important and increasingly central organizing principle.

Church, Cult, and Pueblo Internal Organization

The church is itself formed by a number of sodalities organized into a systemic whole. The concept of cults, which may or may not be incorporated into a church organization, must be introduced here. Churches consist of sodalities, including groups of lay ministers, sacristans, women singers and altar women, fiestero or ceremonial host groups assigned to the cult of the patron saint, and other special sodalities. Associated with the church in a different way are the church governors, appointed by the lay ministers and approved by the heads of families of the pueblo, or congregation, and the former church governors, who form a respected and powerful advisory group. A military or police sodality is under the command of the council in times of peace. Some sodalities are less specifically under the command of any of these units. The *paskolas*, a ritual dance group of aboriginal origin, willingly put their services at the disposal of the pueblo official for a fee paid by the fiestero sodality, or because of a ceremonial promise to the church cult image. Figure 2 summarizes these relationships.

Historical information about Mayo organization during the Revolution of 1910 indicates that in times of war the Mayo social organization is capable of uniting military sodalities from numbers of pueblos under a single paramount war leader. Under a Mayo leader from Bánari, some two thousand Mayos went to battle in the second decade of this century.

The necessary sense of unity for this kind of organizational capacity is provided in large part by a systematic and widespread ceremonial exchange system in which all church and pueblo officials and sodalities participate in varying degrees.

Membership in any given sodality is usually entered into with the formal ritual of a promise, or *manda*, to the saint with whose cult the sodality is associated. All sodalities are associated with the cults of one or more saints. This promise is made by the

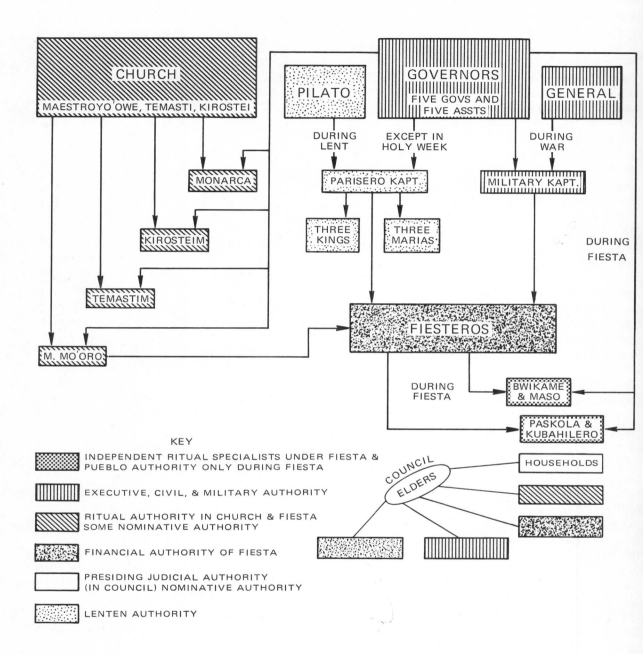

Figure 2. Organizational chart of Mayo social units within the pueblo during intervillage processions.

Arrowed lines indicate direction of authority. Simple lines indicate primarily cooperative, non-authoritative relationships between these groups in other contexts, as in the Pueblo Council.

individual, usually with the counsel and advice of kin and ritual kin. He acquires through the promise an obligation to serve the saint in the capacity of a member of a given sodality in return for the cure of his illness or his preservation from harm through a crucial period. In some sodalities parents perform ritual labor on behalf of children, or anyone may pay a manda on behalf of another. Specific saints are known to be especially able to cure or to protect against certain varieties of diseases, or to guide children safely to adulthood.

In some sodalities there is a tendency to affiliation — that is, children tend to join the same sodalities in the same pueblos of a parent. This tendency seems a natural correlate of an ancestor earth cult combined with localized saints' cults. Fixed lineal descent is positively not required today for participation in any sodality at Bánari, however, and sodalities are not exogamous. Membership of one sodality associated with the cult of the patron saint was addressed by the pueblo officials in a ritual speech as "*Malam, nuhmeame*" (Man speaking, daughters, sons-in-law), and other kin terms are often used in these ritual addresses. Thus we cannot ignore the probability of kinship patterns originally influencing sodality structure and development. Kinship has, however, become secondary to the idea of the sodality itself at present.

Authority and Command

A chart of the command structure of Mayo organization, including the relationship of officials and sodality heads and officers, is included in Figure 2. The internal command of each sodality, such as the military society; the Lenten men's society, the *pariseros*; the large dance society closely associated with the church, the *matachin* society; and all the rest, including each group of church sodalities, is hierarchical in internal organization. Each is characterized by fine differences in rank and insignia and internal division of labor. Such divisions are illustrated for one sodality, the fiesteros of the patron saint of Bánari, in Figure 3.

Exchanges between pueblos are arranged and managed by the heads of various sodalities or officials. Lay ministers and governors arrange more distant and important exchanges, and specific aspects of the actual processions and rituals are delegated to the officers of the matachin society, military society officers below the level of first captain, officers of the

men's Lenten sodality below the level of *Pilato*, and officers of the patron saint fiestero group. The more distant the pueblo with whom the exchange is initiated the more powerful the official who arranges the exchange or initiates it. The matachin *monarca* may take full responsibility for taking the matachin society to dance in households at the Bánari church area, and even to neighboring pueblos close by and in the same municipio. Between very closely related pueblos the *maestro mo?oro*, commander of a patron saint fiestero group, may be the only official in charge of a small exchange. As distance increases, however, and larger groups of sodalities are involved, the *maestro yo?owe*, or head lay minister, may take an actual part in negotiations and the governor and higher ranking officials make initial arrangements and remain in ultimate command.

The Cult System

In Bánari, a small pueblo of the Huatabampo municipio, there is a small church whose patron saint is the *Santisima Tiniran*, and this is one of the central cults of that area. Bánari is unique in having this very particular form of the saint as its patron, and in having its own mythology and unique interpretation and ritual in association with this saint. It is not unique, however, in the fact of having a patron saint, as all Mayo churches do. Furthermore, the cult of this saint is associated with a formalized fiestero or ceremonial host sodality (*paskome*), a matachin dance sodality with an internal hierarchy, and age-grading system, and several other sodalities. Other important cults within the Bánari church are the cults of the crucified Christ, with which a male Lenten sodality (*Pariserom*) is associated; the Christ child, with whom the governors, the military society, the church officials and men of the pueblo are associated, together with the patron saint called the Three Kings, at the season of the Pariserom. The women and children of the pueblo during Lent are dedicated to the Three Marys.

Though the Holy Trinity is the patron saint of Bánari, and thus Bánari is the center of its cult, this image is found also in other churches, just as Bánari has an image of the Holy Cross though the Holy Cross is the patron of a nearby pueblo, Homecarit. Bánari also has an image of Saint John the Baptist, though he is the patron saint of a more distant pueblo, and so on. Give or take an image or two, each Mayo church is a microcosm of the Mayo pantheon in its inventory

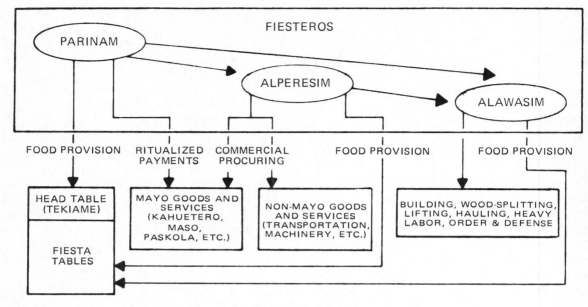

a. DIVISION OF LABOR, ECONOMIC SPHERE.

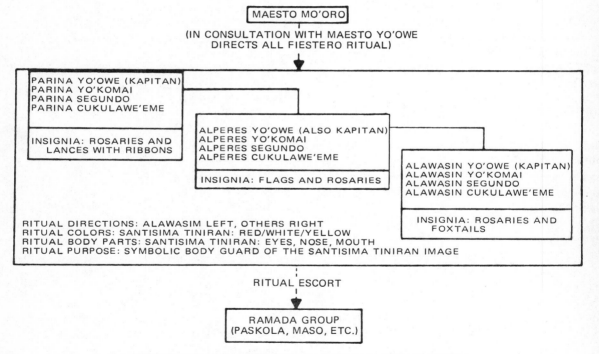

b. DIVISION OF LABOR AND LINE OF COMMAND, RITUAL SPHERE.

Figure 3. Internal organization of a Mayo sodality, the patron saint fiesteros of Bánari, with reference to two spheres of authority: (a) economic and (b) ritual.

of saints, though each church is unique in having a particular patron of its church, and each church is related intimately to its particular patron saint as well as to that group of saints' cults normally found in every Mayo church in much the same form. Lenten cults are a good example of this.

Cults are not always associated with churches exclusively, however. Some saints' images are kept in small chapels near the "owner" or person in connection with whose vision or supernatural experience the cult originated, and who supervises its ritual and in a less formal way the sodalities associated with it. Such cults also have fiestero groups, but they are not organized with insignia and do not involve so much formal ritual as patron saint paskome groups.

There are also patron saints associated with each pueblo. The patron saint of Bánari pueblo is the Holy Cross.

All these kinds of cults integrate people from many communities among the Mayos, however, in addition to intensifying internal community integration. Individuals travel miles to participate in a sodality dedicated to a saint known to cure rare diseases or known to be especially miraculous.

Because of the nature of the causation of sickness, in Mayo belief, all curing of serious illness has divine justification and is backed by divine power. Mayo shamanistic diagnosticians often specialize in curing different types of disease, and have clienteles. These people are believed to have had supernatural experience or dream experience in which they were given *gracia*, or the grace, from some manifestation of God, to enable them to be able to cure a variety of diseases. This power is neither good nor bad, but essentially just powerful. It is through the human will that the power is manifest to punish the witches and sorcerers and relieve the innocent of pain.

The *hitolio*, or curer of diseases caused by witches or sorcerers, has the power to divine the cause of illness in a patient and recommend the proper treatment. He knows this partly by the descriptions of the symptoms, too, but the ideological justification is divine power. One does not go to a curer unless one is very ill in the first place, so his place is a very important one in society. According to his revelation, then, and his knowledge, he recommends his own herbal and spiritual treatment in the case of witchcraft-caused diseases; or, in the case of illnesses said to be sent by God, he normally recommends making a manda to a saint, and he may even specify which saint is good for the illness. In the lower Mayo River valley there have been other remedies and preventative measures used against God-sent diseases, but for the present discussion let us consider the manda-making link between the fiesteros and the hitolio — how it influences the waxing and waning of a given saint's cult. Any given hitolio tends to function as a mechanism in the maintenance of the cults of given saints. His clientele also form a ritual kin group which integrates people across pueblo lines.

The cults which the particular hitolio strengthens may be church cults or household cults. If his supernatural vision in which he first received gracia was an extraordinary one, he may be aided by relatives and compadres in founding a cult associated with his own manifestation of the saint.

Thus the social structures involved in ceremonial exchange are already complexly related and overlapping in terms of the relationships of actual people and ideas they involve. Pueblo, kinship and residence, ritual kinship, church, cults and clienteles, all combine with the more formalized sodalities to produce the complex base on which the next level of distinctively Mayo social integration is built.

2. MECHANISMS OF MAYO SOCIAL INTEGRATION

HOW CEREMONIAL EXCHANGE OPERATES

Definition of Terms

One of the chief integrative mechanisms of inter-community organization among the Mayos is ceremonial exchange. By ceremonial exchange is meant the flow of people in religious roles, of religious information, and of paraphernalia between churches and homes. More specifically, Mayo ceremonial exchange involves movements of the following kind: (1) ceremonial sodalities or individuals who perform rituals connected with the cult or cults of church-based or house-based saints, such groups often having flags and insignia or a distinctive costume which they may use when on pilgrimage; (2) the image of the saint itself, which may be housed in either a church or a small chapel associated with a home; (3) a certain amount and quality of ritual information associated with the cults of the relevant saints.

These basic ingredients of exhange may flow between the following units (Fig. 4): (1) a church and the households whose members are customarily associated with that church, (2) households with or without the interventions of a church, (3) two different churches, and (4) churches and households customarily associated with another and different church.

Almost all possible combinations of the flow of cult personnel (sodalities) and saints occur in Mayo life.

There are two basic varieties of cults, which can also be thought of as the bases for sodalities, and each integrates a different realm of units. The cult implies both a social unit and a set of rituals and beliefs. The home-based saints have their permanent residence in a chapel near the "owner" (ʔápateak), and the social organization of this cult is often based on a ritual kinship or curer-clientele association with the owner of the saint. It integrates households with one another with or without the intervention of a church in the host territory (Fig. 4 B). However, cult leaders and "owners" of saints often tend to become powerful as officials and sodality heads in their own church territories, drawing their own household cults or personal cults into the church network.

Every church-based saint is associated with one or more sodalities, with a rotating membership drawing almost all homes of an area into their roles within a number of years. Particularly closely associated with their saints are the fiestero groups of the patron saints, ceremonial hosts who have insignia, flag, an established and intricate set of rituals, and firm symbolic ties to their particular church and saint. They are the "soldier guard" — the standard bearers, literally — of their saint. Wherever this image goes they go also. Other sodalities, such as the matachin society, which performs a variety of ceremonial dances, and the lay ministers, are all firmly connected in popular ideology and social structure with the churches where their patron saint is located. Together with the congregations of that church, these groups constitute the church in a social sense.

Types of Exchange

In the following section the reader will find reference to Figure 4 particularly helpful in understanding the levels and types of Mayo ceremonial integration, which will be outlined and described briefly.

One of the smallest circles of exchange and perhaps the most intensely meaningful for Mayos is the exchange of church sodalities and saints' images within the church area with the homes of its own territory (Fig. 4 A). Much of this exchange follows a pattern essentially the same for each ceremonial year, though some is involved with unpredictable crisis rites, as is much of the exchange associated with household cults. In church-home exchange, the matachin society, for example, frequently goes out to perform in funeral ceremonies at households in the area of the affiliated church. Before burial of the dead, the home and church groups return together to the church and from there to the cemetery. The cemetery is especially sacred to the group, as an ancestor cult is one

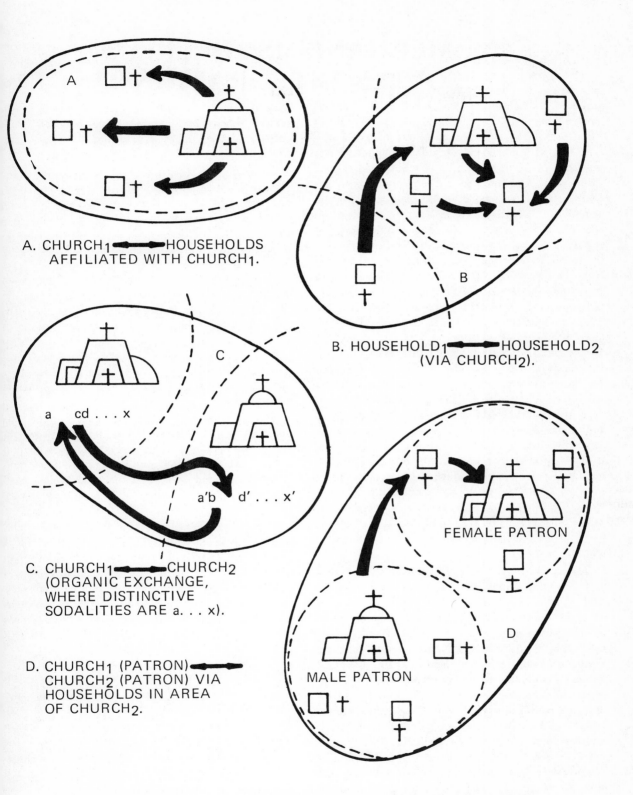

A. CHURCH₁ ◀━━▶ HOUSEHOLDS
AFFILIATED WITH CHURCH₁.

B. HOUSEHOLD₁ ◀━━▶ HOUSEHOLD₂
(VIA CHURCH₂).

C. CHURCH₁ ◀━━▶ CHURCH₂
(ORGANIC EXCHANGE,
WHERE DISTINCTIVE
SODALITIES ARE a. . . x).

D. CHURCH₁ (PATRON) ◀━━▶
CHURCH₂ (PATRON) VIA
HOUSEHOLDS IN AREA
OF CHURCH₂.

Figure 4. Levels of integration effected by some types of Mayo ceremonial exchange.

of the most important cults of each Mayo community and kin group.

The second type of exchange incorporating a church and the households of its own territory involves the exchange of an image as well as its associated sodalities with households within the territory of the church. The Lenten home fiestas in Bánari illustrate this type of exchange. In this example the image of ʔItom ʔAcai ʔUsi (Our Father, Son) is accompanied by several church sodalities — notably a men's Lenten ceremonial sodality, the pariseros, who are symbolically associated with this image. A second example is the series of San Juan home fiestas in Bánari, in which the image of the Santisima Tiniran or Holy Trinity of that village is accompanied to the fiesta household by the Santisima Tiniran fiesteros, who serve for the nativity fiesta of *San Juan Bautista* (Saint John the Baptist) as well as for the Santisima Tiniran in this pueblo. These fiestas are regular calendrical affairs.

The exchanges between a church and its constituent households (Fig. 4 A) form a basic internal integrating mechanism in the Mayo church communities. They provide a vehicle for the spread of information associated with cults of the important local saints, and of the knowledge of formal ritual, myth, and the associated social structures. Since interaction is stronger between a church and the households of its territorial constituents (though church territories in some areas interpenetrate and overlap to some extent), there tends to be a much stronger sense of social unity and shared symbolism within such a community than between this and another Mayo community on the whole.

The cults of the saints predominantly associated with a given community have distinctive myths rooted in local geography and oral history and which are quite different from those associated with saints by the same name in other church communities. Furthermore, the following characteristics are diagnostic of an organic rather than mechanical type of integration: (1) the allocation of authority to heads of sodalities, (2) the forming of all sodalities and family heads within the pueblo into a council for important decisions, (3) the division of labor among sodalities very different from one another in structure and function, and (4) the division of kinds of authority among different officials. The pueblo church and the exchange relationship maintained between it and the

closely surrounding households cements the relationship which takes actual physical form in the council of officials, sodality heads, and household heads.[*] Mayos regard the council as the very basis of earthly authority in their political system, though the ultimate authority of Mayo government and all group activity is recognized as supernatural.

Those are the explanations of Mayos in official statuses, and the structure clearly reflects these analyses. It is not so much that the governors, lay ministers, and other authorities command, as that they coordinate groups with mutually complementary functions. It is clearly understood which group is responsible for what activities during each part of the ceremonial calendar, and appropriate officials have the power to call upon the military or parisero society for police action, should that be necessary. At the community level Mayo social organization is a small city-state with even jural and police authority intimately connected to church or religious authority and all authority subject to veto by the heads of all households, a privilege rarely exercised. Unanimity rather than majority rule, however, is the principle involved here.

Perhaps the most important point about this organization is the nature of dissent. Being essentially egalitarian, as tribal peoples always are, Mayos require a high level of conformity with regard to certain standards of conduct. Disagreements, if fundamental, may lead to serious splits. If reconciliation is impossible after a quarrel, the losing faction may move off and start another village. It does not remain and become a minority part, typically. In recent as well as earlier times not all Mayo villages have been formed as factional groups splitting off from parent villages in this way. For example, economic considerations such as the founding of ejidos as well as farming colonies have been important also. A large number of villages in the Huatabampo municipio have however formed

---

*Spicer (1954, Figure 6, 99-103) witnessed the actual meeting among Potam Yaquis of a pueblo council for purposes of conducting a trial of a church official. As the trial progressed an accused person from another pueblo, Vicam, became involved, so the entire officialdom — a duplicate set of officials and sodalities from the village of the second person — joined the council. In Bánari we were not able to witness a council of this type as none occurred during our stay, but such meetings were described which had occurred recently in the replacement and election of various officials, a matter of sufficient importance to warrant approval of the entire roster of community authority.

originally as factional groups subsequently forming separate churches. Huícori split from Bánari in a dispute, and Tosalipaku split in turn from Huícori. The only pueblo church in this area which seems to have split from its parent pueblo without conflict was Homecarit, and this may reflect only an incomplete historical record.

A much greater integrative task is required of types of intercommunity exchange in bringing together different communities than is required in the internal community integration systems. In the intercommunity exchange system there is a variety of structures. The exchange of sodalities between churches without any accompanying saints (Fig. 4 C) is also a common pattern in the area around Camalobo. This type of exchange draws together people from a wider geographical and social circle than any type of exchange discussed so far. The Santa Kurus (Holy Cross) fiesteros associated with the particular Santa Kurus image at the church of Homecarit, for example, performed Lenten ceremonies with the sodalities at Bánari in the company of Bánari's Santisima Tiniran fiesteros in 1961, assisting in a wide variety of duties for which a formalized Santa Kurus fiestero sodality is felt necessary. Bánari itself did not have a formalized fiestero group of this type in 1961 (Fig. 4 C; sodality b). On the other hand Homecarit did not have a sodality of the type c, in this case a matachin society, so Bánari sent their matachin society to perform at the fiesta of the flag of the Homecarit Santa Kurus for which such a performance is felt essential. In both these cases only sodalities are exchanged between churches by agreement of church officials (lisénsia) — which tends to become traditional in most cases, and no images of saints necessarily accompany them. When an image does not accompany a visiting sodality, this type of exchange certainly appears to signify at least an incipient form of organic integration between churches, because the "borrowed" sodality serves in a capacity complementary to the function of sodalities in the host church.

The exchange of saints along with a large number of associated sodalities between a church and homes in the territory of another and different church (Fig. 4 D) is widespread in the exchange structure. It is usually, however, part of a wider pattern of exchange between two churches. For example, in any of the several patron saint exchanges described in the Camalobo area (Fig. 5), the fiesteros of the host

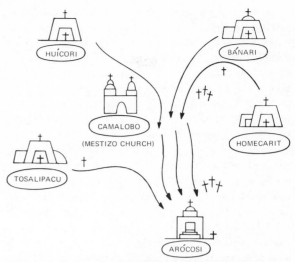

Figure 5. Procession formation of church groups to Arócosi, Espíritu Santu fiesta

church meet the visiting image and fiesteros and escort them to a home in the territory of the host group. They all remain at this household for an interval to rest (hémyori) in the traditional patron saint exchange system. Thus the cults of two different Mayo church saints are integrated through the intermediary of at least one or often more homes in the host territory. Sometimes this occurs through a full pasko of over twenty-four hours, and at other times only through a briefer ceremony of three or four hours. Even a brief ceremony however includes a set of rituals and prayers in the interlude before the entry of the visiting saint and his retinue to the host church proper, together with the offering of water and rest to the pilgrim fiesteros and matachin society before they proceed.

A full and splendid example of the patron saint exchange is maintained between the Mayo churches of Bánari and Arócosi. Bánari goes to Arócosi for the Whitsunday fiesta (seventh Sunday after Easter) of The Holy Spirit. Arócosi then comes to Bánari for the fiesta of the Holy Trinity the following Sunday. In both these exchanges almost the entire structure of sodalities constituting the church communities in both villages take part in the rituals. The heads of various sodalities arrange and manage details of the group pilgrimages, led by matachin dancers, followed by the fiesteros and the patron saint images. The lay ministers, sacristans, singers, and pueblo governor and advisors follow the image closely. At a cross, usually a *kurus yo'owe* (great cross), outside the host village the visiting procession merges with a reception group. It is a maxim of Mayo intercommunity organization that an official of the same sodality and rank always receives a visitor of the same sodality and rank.

On long stretches of road or path where there are no ritual stops, the form of the procession may change from that described above. High officers of the church sodalities, governors, and high pueblo officials may go ahead and arrange for the arrival of the procession. The matachin organization, commanded by the hierarchy of monarcas and officials, and the paskome, commanded on this occasion by an officer of the military society or of the parisero society, follow with the image. Occasionally in some long processions everyone rides in trucks until they reach points at which rituals are customarily held.

In this specific patron saint exchange, the lay ministers of the host and visiting churches greeted one another and remained together, as was also observed in patron saint exchanges between Bánari and Homecarit. Commanders of dance sodalities and fiesteros actually marching with them and directing them said they in turn were under command of the lay ministers and the governors who had made original arrangements. In the procession to Arócosi, as many as 2,000 people marched in the group at times.

Integration of Pueblos Through Patron Saint Exchange — An Example

A brief description of the visit of Bánari Santisima Tiniran to Arócosi on the eve of the Espíritu Santu fiesta of Arócosi in late May of 1961 may illuminate some of the integrative aspects of the church-to-church patron saint exchange system (Figs. 5 & 6).

About 3:00 a.m. on the Saturday preceding the feast day, a procession formed in Bánari, headed by a large group of young men and women being initiated into the matachin society. Mayo girls are generally initiated at this time and promised to the Santisima Tiniran after their first menses. Before this, each one is supposed to have learned to grind corn on a metate with a mano and to have spent a day grinding corn inside the house. The age of the boys participating in the matachin dancing on this day would indicate that it is a similar initiatory ritual for them. Ages of boys and girls we knew were between nine and fourteen. Most were toward the older end of the range. The

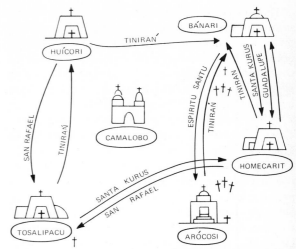

Figure 6. Summary of some patron saint exchanges between five Mayo pueblos.

occasion is explicitly thought of as an initiation for these young people.*

The performing nucleus of the matachin society consists of about seven mature men, who are outstandingly good dancers and who are officers in the society. The head of the society has authority in the church council, though he is under the governors and lay minister in authority. He is called the monarca. There is a group of monarcas under him, ranked by number, segunda (second), tercera (third), and so on. In addition there is an official in the sodality with the title of 'alwasil. He is directly responsible to the monarca and is thought of as an assistant to him. The monarcas lead the dances. When there are new initiates, as during the season described, these officials take charge of the new members and supervise their dancing.

At other times of the year, as on Gloria Saturday (Easter), the little boys and young men of the pueblo dance with the matachin society, and the participating group is very large. No women dance, except for the Tiniran-Espíritu Santu season. The participation of the male members of the society is expected for most of the major fiestas of the year. A rotating nuclear group of mature men, often about seven at a time, expert dancers, generally participates in house fiestas and funerals.

---

*This pattern in general resembles rituals observed by Stevenson (1905: 303-4) among the Zunis. It also resembles Hopi patterns (Stephen 1936: 139-42).

During the season, however, between Whitsunday and the fiesta of Trinity Sunday in 1961 in Bánari, the matachin dancing group was enormous, consisting of some four hundred girls and boys directed by the men who were officers of the sodality. The young people were from many villages surrounding Bánari, but concentrated to this pueblo church on this occasion. The girls marched in a formation separate from and at right angles to the boys. They were directed by a separate monarca. The godmothers or ritual sponsors of the girls went immediately behind the girls, together with several officers of the sodality. Second in the procession were the standard bearers of the Santisima Tiniran, the fiesteros who carry its flag, and the image itself. Beside them were the fiesteros of Homecarit, whose flag went beside that of the Santisima Tiniran. Both fiestero groups were accompanied by their *mo²oros*, ritual specialists directly under the head maestros who supervised the ritual activities (as opposed to the feasting, entertainment, and other activities) of the fiesteros.

This Santa Kurus fiestero group had joined the Bánari Santisima Tiniran group at the point of origin of the main procession in Bánari. The image of the Santisima Tiniran followed the paskola and *maso* ceremonial dance and song groups. These dancers, fundamentally less closely associated with the church in terms of command structure and symbolic meanings, nevertheless always marched closer to images of the saints in processions and seemed more closely related to these images in processions than did any other group except the lay ministers, who immediately follow the images. This is one of the patterns which makes it possible to infer that these dancers probably were part of the system of priesthoods in an earlier stage of Mayo society.

The paskola dancers, usually four or more, and one or two maso dancers, turn backward periodically in a special step during the formal progress of the procession to salute the image of the saint, then they turn and dance forward, leading the image down the procession path. Following the image, as noted, were the church group consisting of lay ministers, sacristans, and women's church sodalities. At the end of the series of sodalities is the group referred to as the church and pueblo government, the church governors and the advisory groups, the former governors and elders.

This procession includes virtually the entire set of sodalities which forms the church of Bánari, organically combined with a complementary sodality from Homecarit, and with a modified form of matachin sodality for this particular event. In this form it progressed on foot from Bánari to Camalobo. On that path, which is intensely sacred to Mayos for mythological and historical reasons, the procession stopped several times to perform prayers and rituals at the pueblo boundary cross of Bánari and at the crosses which mark the places of martyrdom of heroes of mythical significance to the Mayos of Bánari and Homecarit (which shared until recently a common history). It arrived at the edge of the town of Camalobo at about dawn, where it was to merge with a similar procession from Huícori (Fig. 6) after stopping at a few houses.

At Camalobo the composition of the Bánari procession changed. The governmental structure of this city is controlled by non-Mayos and the dancing of the paskola group is forbidden here by municipal law. A group of mariachis and a brass band replaced the two Mayo dance sodalities and the associated Mayo singers and musicians. And the procession continued through a series of highly abbreviated salutes to various crosses and houses throughout the city. On arrival at the mestizo church in Camalobo, the Bánari-Homecarit procession met the Huícori procession in a brief ceremony within the church in which a Mexican Catholic priest exchanged the rosaries of the Santisima Tiniran fiesteros of Bánari with the incoming fiesteros. He performed the same ritual with the Santisima Tiniran fiesteros of Huícori, which has this saint as a patron, though its image and myth differ slightly from that of the Bánari cult. This ritual, symbolizing the official induction of the new fiesteros of the cult to the charge of acting fiestero for one year, lasted about one-half hour.

The procession, now combined with the Huícori procession, which had entered Camalobo in a similar form and series of stops as the Bánari, except following a different procession path to the church, went to a house in one of the Mayo sections of Camalobo, where they performed a brief ceremonial ritual. At this time the church officials and top officials of the sodalities together with the paskola and maso dance and musical groups went ahead of the rest of the procession in trucks. A lower echelon officer of the parisero society, also an officer of the military society, had been appointed by the governors to supervise the part of the procession which would walk from Camalobo to Arócosi. The matachin society, with its officers, the godmothers of the girls, and the girls and boys led the walking group. The fiesteros followed with the image, the supervising official leading them. By the time they arrived at Arócosi this group had walked some twelve or fourteen miles since the origin of their procession in Bánari only a few hours earlier, and they would be expected to return by foot the following day. In addition, the young matachin society initiates would be expected to dance for much of the intervening time, night and day.

The seven miles between Camalobo and Arócosi was done at a very fast walk, at a pace between walking and trotting. The sandal of the commanding captain cut through the flesh between his toes, but he did not stop the procession or slow down to adjust it. The whole attitude of Mayos toward their ceremonial life is that it is a difficult and exacting business and that individual pain and fatigue must not stand in the way of the performance of one's duty as a sodality member, and particularly an official, who must be exemplary. *

During this fast walk of the smaller group to Arócosi the images were wrapped in the cloths normally used to shade them from the sun in processions — "wrapped for the road."

As the groups neared Arócosi around 9:00 a.m., two women came to meet the images, one crawling on her knees and the other scattering water from side to side out of a narrow mouthed bottle as she advanced down the path toward the images.† The procession was then met by two sets of fiesteros who had come out from Arócosi, the ⁷Espíritu Santu fiesteros, of Arócosi, and the *San Rafael* fiesteros of Tosalipacu. A welcoming ritual and a formal speech inviting the group into the host pueblo preceded the reformation of a complex procession incorporating all five pueblos, rejoined now by almost all the involved

sodalities, some of whom had preceded the procession. This included paskola and maso dancers and musicians, all church and pueblo officials, and so on. This recombination of groups took place at the entrance of the pueblo where three reception crosses were placed. The image of ⁷Espíritu Santu was brought out by a large Arócosi procession. This image was dipped in greeting to the two visiting images of the Santisima Tiniran, and each of the three images was rested at one of the three crosses. This moment in ceremonial exchanges, at which the guest and host images meet, is invariably called by Mayos, "The meeting of Our Father and Our Mother" (or "greeting" or "embrace"). [⁷*Itom* ⁷*Acai* ⁷ *into* ⁷*Itom* ⁷*Aye* ⁷*omom nankenake*; ⁷*omom tebotúanake*; ⁷*omom* ⁷*ibáktianake*. "Our Father and Our Mother meet one another; greet one another; embrace one another".] In this case ⁷Espíritu Santu is Our Mother and Santisima Tiniran is Our Father.

The enormous procession now proceeded to a house in the territory of the host church, where the image was received on a small house altar in the ramada of the house in a series of rituals lasting about an hour. The pilgrim sodalities were offered water after the matachin society danced for some time in a formation the shape of a cross. The girls danced in two lines parallel to the ramada, and the boys danced in two lines at right angles to them, moving through the lines of girls from time to time.

Meanwhile the fiesteros and the lay ministers performed a short ceremony at the altar, the fiesteros performed a long and complex flag-waving ritual involving all five fiestero groups at the houseyard cross, and then rested. After the hemyori, or ritual rest stop, the entire amalgamation of sodalities from all five Mayo pueblos proceeded to the Arócosi church for a further series of rituals after a few hours.

By describing the progress of this procession during less than the course of one morning, one can illustrate the integration of sodalities from five Mayo pueblos. Camalobo church is excluded because it does not participate in patron saint exchange, contributing neither sodalities nor images — two of the diagnostic ingredients of Mayo ceremonial exchange. It is today a mestizo church, though formerly it was the site of an important Mayo church now abandoned.

---

*This is a manifestation of the same orientation which Spicer (1954: 177-81) terms a "ceremonial labor" orientation for Potam Yaquis.

†Padre Mendez (Perez de Rivas 1944: 14) reported that his group was greeted in a similar way when they went into the villages of Nebomes to get corn and supplies for feeding other newly missionized people in the Cahitan area. Also, a similar ritual was formerly practiced in the Mayo area as a part of a rain ceremony.

SUMMARY OF TYPES OF CEREMONIAL EXCHANGE DESCRIBED

The significance of a distinction between household and church cults has not yet been fully demonstrated, but such a distinction has been made on two accounts. One is that the distinction will help us to understand the historical stages of Mayo organizational development as household cults, or something resembling them may be assumed to have preceded church cults. The other is that the distinction helps us to recognize the social foundations of charismatic leadership, especially that involving shaman and prophet, types of leadership usually associated with what at least begins as household cults, though this leadership may through time come into various churches and become established as a church cult. Such a developmental sequence can be documented for some Mayo cults. The distinction between household and church cults helps, however, to distinguish charismatic leaders from those with established and police-sanctioned authority, backed by community and church government resting in turn on the authority of the major saints' cults recognized from time immemorial, according to general Mayo belief. Household cults, in contrast, are less generally supported.

Five exchange flows have been briefly described, illustrating levels and units of integration between these types of cults. These can be put in shorthand in the following way:

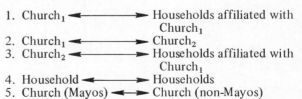

1. Church$_1$ ←———————→ Households affiliated with Church$_1$
2. Church$_1$ ←———————→ Church$_2$
3. Church$_2$ ←———————→ Households affiliated with Church$_1$
4. Household ←———————→ Households
5. Church (Mayos) ←———→ Church (non-Mayos)

Church-to-church exchange has been developed most fully, since in the patron saint exchange system, for example, most of the other exchange flows are incorporated as elements.

Additional explanation of why it is useful to distinguish these types is in order. Especially the relationship of Mayo to mestizo churches remains to be clarified. We will show in the following chapter that this is not the same kind of relationship that prevails between Mayos in Mayo churches, as it lacks the basic social elements of exchange characteristic of Mayo pueblo relationships and household ceremonial exchange relationships and as its forms have different symbolic values for the non-Mayos of Camalobo church than for the Mayos of the village churches.

3. ANALYSIS OF EXCHANGES AS INTEGRATIVE MECHANISMS

ETHNIC INTEGRATION

Integration of Mayo Units with Other Mayo Units

The type of Mayo church-to-church exchange illustrated by the Bánari-Arócosi exchanges involves a more-or-less mechanical combination of large numbers of sodalities. But it also incorporates, in this case, church-to-household exchanges (types 2 and 3, above). It forms a chain of relationships between whole communities through their native church organizations. Though this integration of native churches fluctuates over a period of decades, according to informants, it tends to become traditional and forms one of the important mechanisms of Mayo tribal unity.

Adding to ceremonial exchange as a mechanism of tribal integration is the composition of sodalities. The fiestero group of any given church patron saint, for example, tends to be made up of individuals from a much wider geographical area than the church in which it serves. In 1960 and 1961 fiesteros in Bánari came from Camalobo and a large number of other pueblos in the lower Mayo River valley as well as from several communities on the Fuerte River to the South in Sinaloa. Bánari people claim that this is because their image is very powerful and has performed many miraculous cures.

Kinship and ritual kinship ties are also important in this process, for parents and ritual kin recommend and direct their children and godchildren to the saints who have cured some other member of the group at an earlier time. This process, not very systematic, but rather liberally interfered with by individual motivations, helps guide the filling of status positions in sodalities. Since shaman curers generally develop ritual kin relationships with their clientele, in connection with their curing as well, they find opportunities to influence considerably the sodalities and cults to which their ritual kin become promised.

Thus there are many mechanisms of intercommunity integration above ceremonial exchange, and on which it may ultimately depend. Nevertheless ceremonial exchange is a useful concept with which to explore the nature of inter-ethnic relationships, for example.

The relationship of the Mayo churches to other Mayo churches as against the mestizo church of Camalobo needs to be clarified. Some essential elements of Mayo ceremonial exchanges of all types include: (1) the face-to-face encounter and salute of the host image and the visiting image (when an image is involved, as it always is in patron saint exchanges) at the pueblo boundary cross of the host village on arrival and farewell of the visiting cortege; (2) reciprocity between the two pueblos with regard to patron saint exchange; (3) a full fiesta or hemyori ceremony for the visiting saint in the host community; (4) detailed ritual speeches in Mayo and ritual routines such as flag-waving and marching of fiestero groups, exchanges of paraphernalia between fiestero groups of visiting and host saints at the pueblo boundary cross (in the patron saint exchange system, and similar rituals at houseyard crosses where hemyori or other house fiestas are held, and at the altars and church crosses of the host pueblos); (5) participation of distinctively Mayo sodalities and particularly of ceremonial dancers known as paskola and maso, who are associated by Mayos with Mayo ceremonial life as distinct from that of mestizos; (6) processions including the image and its fiesteros, Mayo church officials and lay ministers, sacristans, singers and musicians, and the matachin society, as well as paskolas and maso; (7) fireworks; (8) following the procession, common ceremonial feasting of all formal participants as well as the congregations, with the eating in prescribed ways of traditional Mayo foods on Mayo village church grounds; (9) common understandings about the purpose of the entire ceremony and its many ritual segments, including reverence for its mythological charter or base.

There are regular exchanges throughout the year between the Mayo pueblos of Bánari and Homecarit,

Homecarit and Tosalipacu, Tosalipacu and Huícori, as well as the one partially described between Bánari and Arócosi, in which all these essential elements are met. The reciprocal exchanges between Bánari and Arócosi alone ultimately involve the systematic contact of over seven hundred people who are actually participating formally in the sodalities and officials in the exchange. This estimate assumes about 150 paskome, about 50 church and pueblo officials and about twice as many lower echelon military society officials and pariseros under their command; about 25 paskola and maso dancers, musicians and singers together with their managers; about 10 lay ministers, sacristans, mo?oros, and other miscellaneous church sodality heads. It is a conservative estimate. Of course many relatives accompany these people, and a large congregation of informal participants take part also. All of these seven hundred, however, actually perform rituals at some point or other during this exchange.

The guests and relatives bring the total of involved individuals to five or six thousand, coming from all parts of the Mayo country and outside its margins. Furthermore, not necessarily the same people come to the Whitsunday fiesta as to the Trinity Sunday fiesta. Perhaps a quarter or more of these are non-Mayos or mestizoized people not necessarily sharing the meanings common to Mayos. Nevertheless, the rituals and the forms of the sodalities — the total pattern of the activities — exclude non-Mayos and re-enforce Mayo solidarity. Mestizo vendors who come to these fiestas have no ceremonial functions and are openly disapproved of by a large number of Mayos. Carnival attractions which come to both these fiestas are tolerated with little patience by conservative Mayos. Selling for a profit on the ground of the church is felt to be an explicit violation of Mayo custom and law, which require that entertainment (dancing and music) and food be supplied free of cash charges to all participants and guests at a ceremony as a part of the obligation of the fiestero sodality. Obligation to return the food in kind then binds host and guest. Cash is a threat to this relationship. That kind of giving is not only the duty but the right of the fiesteros. The most violent opposition to the presence of non-Mayo vendors at fiestas was heard from fiesteros. By feeding many people the fiestero discharges his promise to the saint for having cured him. The more people who come to a fiesta the more prestige is attached to being a fiestero of the cult. The Santisima Tiniran of Bánari is currently such a grand cult.

Signifance of a Fiesta Type of Distribution in Mayo Ceremonial Exchange

It is clear that a special kind of economic distribution is felt by Mayos to be associated with a religious system in the context of the fiesta, and it is furthermore indicated that interference with that native distribution system is judged to be a threat to the religious system. However, only the changes directly interfering with religious life or with sacred orientations of Mayo culture are strongly resisted. For example, new all-weather roads opening up into the Bánari area in 1961 were at first opposed by some church and pueblo officials on the grounds that they would facilitate the movement of heavy carnival equipment to Bánari for the Trinity Sunday fiesta. Others pointed out that fresh water could be brought out to the village when the water level was high and the wells salty. Bánari subsequently received a water storage tank and piped water.

Mayo technology, or the technology of those who call themselves Mayos, is today characterized by the previously listed contrasts between an early level and later level technology.

The main production units are still the household residence unit and the local community, though both have been modified. The means of production are changing swiftly, and the items produced are often sold commercially rather than distributed directly. This is true in fishing and cattle-raising villages as well as farming villages. But the items produced, though they have changed from food crops to cash crops in agricultural areas, in all areas remain comparatively closely related to products and industries characterizing Mayo exploitation of those areas for many centuries. Nevertheless, the extent to which Mayos are being brought into the Mexican market economy as a result of changes in techniques of production and marketing, and to some extent in the social organization of production, especially as regards the relationships of ejidos and bank-financing arrangements, has also indirectly affected the fiesta distribution system.

Some of the changes are more apparent than real, as money income is frequently brought home and distributed in the household and ultimately among relatives and ritual kin for fiestas, just as food would have been. The two elements so highly valued in the Mayo economic system — primary resources (land, food, and so on) and human labor — continue to have great value. Of these elements the human labor is one

of the most crucial in the continuation of the ceremonial system, for ultimately the goods of exchange
may be bought, but ritual labor must be performed
by the individual or in some cases by a close relative
who may serve on his behalf.

It is in the importance of food distribution and the
labor involved — both in a ritual and physical sense —
that Mayo economic life relates most closely to Mayo
religious life and becomes the very root of the church
and ceremonial system.

Amounts of money spent by fiesteros in giving
these fiestas, and the worth of goods expended in
terms of animals slaughtered, food donated, money
spent, man-hours of work in chopping fuel and building structures, and woman-hours of cooking and
dish-washing — not to mention months and months
out of each year's work time spent in purely ritual
but hard physical labor such as prayer, marching,
flag-waving, and dancing — total without a doubt the
greatest expenditure of resources by any given fiestero participant in any other activity during the
whole year. Spending participation in the Mexican
economy on the other hand involves the buying of
seeds, clothes, cooking vessels, and for some families,
bicycles, radios, utilities (electricity, and now for
some pueblos, water). In addition, all farmers on irri-
gated lands are required to pay road and canal taxes,
and irrigation costs. Some Mayo craft products, in
turn, are marketed through the Mexican market
system.

There is a well-established system of cash exchange
within Mayo culture also. Some Mayo craft products
and services for which there is little demand outside
Mayo society are exchanged between families and
groups using cash as a medium of exchange, often in
the context of a fiesta, when services and products of
dance specialists, fireworks makers, and other specialists are arranged for. But there is often a highly formalized and distinctively Mayo pattern to such exchange which sets it apart from the relatively impersonal mestizo or non-Mayo patterns in use in the
Mexican market system. Usually noticeable is that
Mayo exchange is an exchange between groups rather
than individuals, with formal speeches about the
meaning and purpose of the exchange.

Though actual behavior deviates some from the
rule, an ideal pattern states that fiesta food, as against
other items and services, should not be bought and
sold. Three main groups of sacred foods could be said
to symbolize or at least be characteristic of the three
Mayo ecological zones: (1) *wakabaki*, or beef stew —
probably formerly *masobaki*, or deer stew — and *hisobare*, loin roasted on skewers, parallel the forest areas;
(2) corn foods, including *bannari*, or a corn mush
drink often sweetened with home-produced honey,
abari, corn roasted on the cob, represent the agricultural areas along the river; (3) a long list of coastline
products, including fish and shell fish, especially
important in Holy Week and central to the daily pro-
tein intake, as well as salt. Salt is always an important
foodstuff and medium of exchange, as well as a ceremonial item involved in crisis rites and rites of intensification.

The seasons, in addition to ecological zones, are
related to ritual foods. *Totoribaki*, or chicken stew, is
associated with San Juan, as are watermelons (*sakobari*). In aboriginal times the turkey may have been
the fowl associated with some similar summer fiesta.
In the fall *kowinohim*, or pork tamales, are made for
the Day of All Saints, and offered to the dead with
fruit, flowers, candles, and water. Before the era of
pigs of the type brought by the Spanish, wild java-
linas probably supplied meat for a fiesta near this
time of the year. Corn is roasted whole for the early
December fiestas, the first ears being brought from
the field of the head governor and eaten ceremoni-
ally, just as in many other Southwestern pueblos.
Bannari and corn foods are again especially closely
associated with Christmas, and fish and loaves of
bread with Lent.

The ritual elaboration of food symbolism, the fer-
tility associations of Mayo religious life, the connection between the earth mother (associated with the
church) and the foods of her body, all relate to a land
and primary resources orientation. The land orientation articulates with the ceremonial labor orientation
in the religion. The attachments of certain saints with
certain foods, flowers, and vegetable products, as well
as certain kinds of curing abilities, are important.
Mayos dedicate a fiesta distribution system to these
saints and a system of value orientation requiring
generosity of food and labor. In this way the value
for food remains opposed, ideologically speaking, to
the exchange of other goods such as clothes, blankets,
mats, and more durable goods. These items may well
have been exchanged in a relatively secularized
though thoroughly Mayo system before hispanic
times, as they appear to be today.

It is interesting that such a deep relationship between primary resources, human labor, and religious life should prevail so strongly today among Mayos even in the face of rapid adaptive changes in the last thirty years toward an individualized, secularized economic pattern. Most Mayo households encourage their members to put surplus into the fiesta system, to invest in obligations while distributing perishable goods. It is an ethic which non-Mayos in the area do not understand fully and which they relate mainly to a condition of relative poverty among Mayos. Mestizo churches do not therefore share its symbolic or social meanings and do not participate in feast exchange with Mayo churches.

In addition to involving economic differences, the relationship between Mayo and mestizo churches is not the same as that which prevails between Mayo churches for these reasons: It lacks other basic social and ritual elements of ceremonial exchange characteristic of Mayo church relationships. Also its forms and meanings have different symbolic values for the mestizos of Camalobo church, for example, than for the Mayos of the village churches.

Mayo-Mestizo Integration

In the yearly round perhaps the most impressive visit of the Bánari Mayo church to the Camalobo mestizo church is involved with the march to Arócosi for the ʔEspíritu Santu fiesta, to which we have already referred. It is at this time that the rosaries of the Santisima Tiniran fiesteros are exchanged. Transfer of ritual information is therefore involved here, though most of the other elements that characterize Mayo ceremonial exchange are missing. Foremost among these is reciprocity, for no saint, no sodality, no priest, not even individuals identified with the Camalobo church, had been regularly invited to Bánari in some decades, nor were they particularly welcome there. Mayos who live in Camalobo go to one of the outlying Mayo churches if they wish to maintain their Mayo identity, rather than to the mestizo church. Reciprocity is characteristic of Mayo church-to-church exchange, on the other hand.

Camalobo church also lacks a church patio cross. Most of the houses at which the image of the Santisima Tiniran was briefly rested in the 1961 procession as it passed on its way to the church also lacked house crosses. Therefore a large number of the characteristically Mayo rituals which center about these crosses simply could not go on.

Paskola and maso ceremonial dance groups and their musicians, essential in all processions involving traditional Mayo patron saint exchanges, on reaching the town of Camalobo, were replaced by mariachis and a brass band. This was necessary because these Mayo dancers were forbidden by municipal law to perform in that town. Fireworks were not used for the same reason. Rest stops of the image in Camalobo were abbreviated to a shadow of the traditional ceremony.

In the Camalobo church no ceremonial host or fiestero sodality now exists, apparently, who considers it a proper and fitting part of their duties, or no Mayo group has the authority to welcome the visiting church personnel as they arrive in the pueblo, or to give the traditional rituals and speeches so important in Mayo ceremonial exchange. There is also no ceremonial feasting or distribution of food between Camalobo as a church and any other Mayo church, and no salute of images face to face, since no images from Camalobo go out in such processions.

In short, a very different kind of basic relationship characterizes the exchanges between the Camalobo mestizo church and the Mayo churches from that among the Mayo churches themselves. The excluding of the Camalobo church from the tribal grouping of churches is no more apparent to anyone than to Mayos themselves, for it was not always so. They describe a somewhat differently integrated pattern of ceremonial exchange before the 1910 Revolution when there was only one church in Camalobo and it still housed Mayo images and Mayo sodalities. Mayos are highly aware, then, of the integrative aspects of Mayo ceremonial exchange patterns, of an economic ethic associated with them, and of which churches are included and excluded in the exchange pattern of any given church.

The varieties of Mayo ceremonial exchange are performed in definite ways and with certain common understandings that largely exclude non-Mayo churches. On the other hand these exchanges integrate Mayo churches into a chain of relationships incorporating increasingly larger numbers of groups and sodalities up to what might be called a tribal level.

In peacetime because the organization appears to be dominantly characterized by a chainlike integrative pattern combining like units or identical sets of sodalities on the intercommunity level, with few exceptions, the dominant integrative type would seem to be what Durkheim calls mechanical.

THE NATURE OF INTEGRATION ACHIEVED IN PATRON SAINT EXCHANGE

Mechanical Social Integration

The patron saint exchange system, as illustrated in the Arócosi-Bánari exchange, is mechanical in the sense that two pueblos combine almost part for part through the entire list of sodalities. Internal pueblo organization is not mechanical; it consists of a cooperative council system linking groups with mutually complementary types of authority and rights and duties. Authority is hierarchical within each sodality, but it is looser between sodalities, though there is also some degree of hierarchical authority here too. The highest authorities are the head maestros, governors, and the elders and former officials. The authority of the elders as presiding officials of a council of household heads in the native judicial system has been enormously eroded by the presence of Mexican legal officials and the breakdown of the earlier landholding system. What is felt to be the full number of elders does not exist in Bánari today because of these facts.

In periods of peace no such hierarchical interpueblo government seems to exist, or at least to meet regularly. Charismatic leadership arises through shaman-clientele organizations which gain leadership across pueblo lines through house-to-house ceremonial exchange of a cult image. Often such a cult gains the support of the officials of a pueblo, and may be incorporated into church ritual there. Two or three such organizations in recent Mayo history have activated tribal unifying forces. The military sodalities may have been formerly headed by warrior-shamans integrating units across pueblo boundaries in a similar way. Definite titles and statuses for the war leaders of the Revolution of 1910 commanding up to two thousand men from several pueblos would indicate that recently there may have been some regular system of promotion to a status of military chieftain above a pueblo-wide level. Approval of pueblo officials in joint meetings or multi-pueblo councils may well have been required.

Complementarity of Cultural Patterns

By making a distinction, however, between social structure and cultural pattern, what appears to be a mechanical integration of pueblo church units becomes considerably more complex. Each pair of patron saints in the patron saint exchange system is complementary in function. Each meeting is called "The meeting of Our Father and Our Mother." The dominant cults of pairs of pueblos require each other for the full performance of the cult ritual of their own respective patron saints. The complementarity thus achieved is a cultural complementarity, somewhat like that described by Fortes (1936) among African Gold Coast groups, a ritual polarity of groups within a ceremonial organization. In the case he describes the rituals are esoteric and the groups were formerly traditional enemies. Fortes suggests that,

Here, perhaps is a clue to the problem of why ritual forms and religious situations should be the institutional media selected for the expression of the equilibrium in Tale society. They have a compulsive power which a pragmatic institution oriented to the demands of the objective world could never have (Fortes 1936: 602).

He further theorizes that the equilibrium achieved in this way forms a barrier to the diffusion of the esoteric rites of one community to another.

The Mayo situation is not fully comparable with the Tale. The Tale social units under discussion are lineages, highly structured kinship descent units, whereas the Mayo units are pueblo church units strongly tied in with patron saint cults. The basis of Mayo social consolidation is not descent as such, but sodality — a key point.

There is, however, a fundamental similarity in that while the social units are alike in structure, their cultural content is complementary. This alone is sufficient to forge them into a single society. The pueblo church of Bánari possesses the cult ritual of the Santisima Tiniran, within which resides the symbolic mate of ⁷Espíritu Santu, whose cult ritual in turn is possessed by the pueblo church of Arócosi. It is through the demands of the saints that Arócosi and Bánari are brought together twice yearly. It is through the complementarity of functions in the pair of symbols rather than in the social structures of Bánari and Arócosi as such.

Cult Segmentation

There are numerous instances demonstrating the mechanisms through which Mayo segmentation and fission result in the founding of new pueblo-church groups. One of the bitterest and most significant splits about which information could be acquired was in the Santisima Tiniran cult. Two cults subsequently resulted.

It appears on the basis of present knowledge that replacing genealogical segmentation is a kind of local cult segmentation and that higher levels of organization, instead of being based on higher lineage levels, are adjusted to the relations between the saints. Thus the cult structure provides, for Mayos, the native rationale for social consolidation, just as a lineage system does for the Tiv or Nuer, for example.

Segmentary sociability, to use Sahlins (1961) phrase, is expressed in terms of explicit rituals – the ritual exchange of paraphernalia or of food and drink, usually between the two groups or their representatives. This ensures the good will of participants toward one another. Presumably ill will – or "bad heart," to put it in Mayo terms – is guarded against in this way. In the Bánari visit to Arócosi for the fiesta of the ⁷Espíritu Santu, for example, the fiesteros of Santisima Tiniran and ⁷Espíritu Santu exchange ceremonial insignia and flags, the banners of their saints, on the first day of their arrival.

The *mo⁷oro*, also called drummer, who is a ritual assistant to the head maestro, directs and leads the fiesteros through all rituals. Persons in this role stood in the center of the group in the May 1961 ⁷Espíritu Santu exchange and, together with the head sacristan, directed the exchange. Fiestero sodalities from at least five pueblos were involved, two Santisima Tiniran cult groups (Bánari and Huícori), a Santa Kurus cult group (Homecarit), and ⁷Espíritu Santu cult group (Arócosi), and a San Rafael cult group (Tosalipacu). A sixth fiestero group, unidentified by the researchers, was present. It may have been the Santa Kurus group of Arócosi, though this is not certain.

The sodalities were arranged so that the ranks within each sodality were grouped together, parinam facing parinam, alawasim facing alawasim, and so on. The pueblos from Etchojoa municipality were at opposite sides of the formation from those of Huatabampo municipality. Higher ranking fiesteros from the municipality of Huatabampo (Huícori, Bánari, and Homecarit) were lined up on one side of a square formation. At right angles to them, the lower ranking fiesteros of their group formed a second line. Facing the higher ranking fiesteros of this group were the parallel group from the municipality of Etchojoa (Arócosi, two groups of fiesteros; and the San Rafael group from Tosalipacu).

Fiesteros then came forward to face each other in pairs, one pair at a time. First the lances, with ribbons appropriate to the official colors of the patron saint, were exchanged by the identical ranks. Fiesteros knelt while the actual exchange took place. They encircled each other's head three times with the paraphernalia before giving it to the member of the opposite group. Next the lowest ranking fiesteros exchanged foxtails, their insignia, tying them on the other person at the waist, as they are customarily worn. When a fiestero did this there was much tension and nervous laughter in the crowd. Some seemed in such a hurry that they tied the foxtail on the other fiestero in what looked more like a wrestling match than a religious ritual. At last the flag-bearers knelt pair by pair and exchanged flags. After each exchange the pair crossed themselves and returned to their positions in the formation.

All the fiesteros had placed blankets before them on the ground. On these blankets were loaves of bread strung together on a rope, punctuated occasionally with oranges, limes, and squashes. These are known as "bread rosaries" (*panim nakúliam*). The fruits and vegetables symbolize the flowers, or tassels, and the bread represents beads. Bread formed the crosses also. Again the fiesteros stepped out by pairs and went to the center, crossed themselves and knelt. Then each threw his string over the other's left shoulder or tried to throw it around the other person's neck. If someone was successful in doing this the person who received the bread rosary took it off quickly. Then the two arose and crossed themselves. This went on until all the bread was exchanged. Finally the drummers (maestro mo⁷oro) and the sacristans exchanged bread rosaries. Then the group marched in a characteristic formation around the large cross (kurus yo⁷owe) of the churchyard and entered the church to formally end this segment of ritual with fireworks. This process was repeated on the departure of the fiesteros from Bánari on the following week.

Now the significance of this ritual is that it demonstrates how segmentary sociability is expressed in ritual opposition and exchange of ceremonial objects between the ritually opposed groups. The three sodalities resident in pueblos of Huatabampo municipality are ritually opposed to the three from Etchojoa municipality. They must be cemented together formally before the common undertaking of fiesta duties.

Similar though less lengthy and detailed rituals cement Bánari and Homecarit when they are combined in patron saint exchanges; Homecarit and Tosalipacu are thus paired; Tosalipacu and Huícori are also paired. The incoming members of each of the patron saint fiestero groups are initiated during these occasions by the outgoing members in fundamentally similar rituals. All such rituals, like the bread exchange, are called "rosaries." The Mayo word for rosary is *nakúlia*, literally change or exchange. Nakuliam for different occasions involve the ceremonial offering of water between paired ranks, the ceremonial smoking of cigarettes lighted from coals in a pottery effigy, and an ingenious list of expressions of reciprocity.

Thus we have a systematic pattern of segmentation expressed in this kind of ritual re-enforced by pueblo and municipality and cult allegiance patterns. The strength of the bond between members of a church's patron saint cult is greatest. This unity is reinforced by the organic internal organization and the relationship between households and church within that unit. But we can demonstrate that between these units, across pueblo and church boundaries, there exists an opposition between patron saint cults. An adaptation from Evans-Pritchard's diagram for showing the way the principle of segmentation operates in Nuer lineages (Evans-Pritchard 1940: 144) can be made for Mayo cult consolidation.

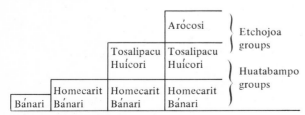

In general the Mayo cult segmentation and fission system are much like lineage segmentation in the sense that groups tend to mass together in proportion to recency of fission and geographical distance. As the diagram shows, there is some confusion as to the identity of Tosalipacu. In the ⁷Espíritu Santu rosary exchange the Arócosi lay ministers grouped Tosalipacu with Arócosi, on the basis that the group is resident in Echojoa municipality. The Huatabampo group was not happy with this classification, as they considered Tosalipacu a Huatabampo cult. In its history of segmentation, it divided from Huícori after Huícori had split from Bánari. Thus the ambivalence of classification of this group derives from the fact that the two criteria which determine massing — recency of fission and geographical distance — conflict in this case.

The full form and extent of the ceremonial exchange system throughout the entire Mayo country was not mapped in this much detail. Many types of ceremonial exchange are probably inherently less patterned than the patron saint system. Exchanges of images occur in both homes and churches between Bánari and Totorim, the northernmost Mayo pueblo on the Mayo River; between Homecarit and a pueblo on the Mocorito River south of the Fuerte River; between Mayo River and Fuerte River pueblos; and between Yaquis and Mayos in a wider Cahitan system. Such exchanges also demonstrate that simple expression of segmentary opposition in terms of cults alone is not easily identified or ritualized in all exchanges, especially in exchange of household saints.

There are other important ways in which the Mayo system differs from segmentary lineage systems such as those of Tiv and Nuer society. Leadership is not entirely relative. On the pueblo level it takes the form of a council comprised of sodality heads. On the inter-pueblo level it takes the form of pueblo-church councils combined in an additive way (e.g., pan-tribal sodalities integrated together) often reinforced by shamanistic charismatic leaders whose power emanates at first from household cults which crosscut many church territories.

In summary, Mayo cult organization resembles segmentary lineage organization in a number of its principles. But it is characterized by sodality integration above kinship integration.

4. AN EXPLANATION OF MAYO SOCIAL ORGANIZATION IN TERMS OF CULTURAL ECOLOGY

SUCCESSION OF PERIODS

Subtract the mestizo-dominated urban centers and their satellite officials and policemen and you have in the Mayo River Valley a modified but recognizable tribal-like Mayo organization. Indeed a late tribal form appears, in some characteristics, to have been crystallizing into a more complex kind of organization before interference in 1890 blocked its development in that direction. It remains, though enclaved in a state, a separate society with a distinct history.

The following chapter encapsulates some of that history in terms of information on (1) population changes and settlement pattern, (2) changes in economic organization and land-holding systems, (3) levels of social organization of enemy groups, (4) situations of war or peace and methods of conducting war and negotiating or maintaining peace, (5) forms of social organization and integrative mechanisms, (6) native leadership and later leadership in the contact organizations when relevant to directed change, (7) religious cults or churches throughout the periods, and (8) system of cultural orientations.

These are precisely the categories in terms of which Spicer (1961: 1-93) has handled the explanation of Yaqui development to illuminate processes of change in Yaqui social and cultural organization as these relate primarily to conditions of contact. Many of the processes that he documents for Yaquis also hold true for Mayos, for there are only few and unimportant differences in Yaqui and Mayo social organizations and cultures, certainly until the beginning of the Relocation Period in 1887. A few differences in the historical events up to the 1880's have helped shape that culture and society up to the present period. Almost every single major event of Yaqui contact history had the same or greater impact on Mayos, often no more than three years to a decade sooner or later.

No attempt will be made here to compare Yaqui and Mayo history and sociocultural structure in any great detail, for it would result largely in a repetition of what has already been done (Spicer 1961: 1-93; 1962: 46-85, 394-405, 529-30) and related specifically to a frame of cultural evolution (Spicer 1962: 371-586). The concept of cultural evolution which Spicer uses incorporates human environment as a variable of increasing importance relative to increasingly complex levels of sociocultural integration. Human environment he expresses in a theoretical system of finely differentiated and classified contact conditions in which social structural (including residence and political units), economic, and cultural (including religious) variables are expressed, and in which articulations between groups are traced out in regard to all these aspects. He deals with the enclaved but distinctive sociocultural units and traces through four centuries the persistence and changes in their identities as each case relates differentially to the contact cultures. In this context, history is primarily a means to the end of understanding the persistence of cultural identities and changes in the social and cultural organization in each individual case, and to explore for underlying similarities in processes.

The concept and method correspond closely to that envisioned by Steward (1955: 30-42) and which he calls "cultural ecology."

Even though technological adaptations may be effects rather than causes of basic adaptations, Steward recommends (1955: 40) the analysis of technological adaptations and their relationship to the environment, or more accurately speaking, to the relevant features of the environment. Secondly he advocates an analysis of the behavior patterns by which people exploit their particular environment by means of their particular technology. Here he recognizes the importance of the development of group efforts. And thirdly, Steward's concept of cultural ecology involves the effect upon other aspects of culture entailed by the behavior patterns arising out of adaptation to the environment.

Because features of human environment, that is, of societies in contact, vary in relative sizes, power, exploitative abilities, and so on, it becomes of special importance with increasing levels of sociocultural integration to evolve a more complex theory of culture contact. For this we need the type of culture change and social change theory employed by Spicer (1954b, 1962 passim).

There are essentially only two approaches to the explanation of the phenomena of culture change in contact situations. On the one hand, such changes are often explained with reference to the nature of the cultures which, through their bearers, come into contact. On the other hand, they are sometimes explained with reference to the conditions of contact. The first approach makes use of concepts such as compatibility, integration, complexity and patterning. The second makes use of concepts such as directed change, social cultural fusion, participation, firsthand contact, intensity of contact, hostility, and duration. It would seem that both approaches are necessary. (Spicer 1954b: 675-6)

In the preceding chapters we have dealt with Mayo integration, complexity, and patterning, making use of concepts appropriate to the first approach. This chapter contains materials for analysis of the second type that Spicer is talking about, and partially summarizes that which he has already done for Cahitan culture.

Prehispanic Periods

Two prehispanic periods are postulated here: an early one, possibly extending backward in time from 1000 A.D. as a purely arbitrary date, and a later one. Much of what is said about the early period is reconstructed from statements in Obregon's history by early Spanish explorers (Hammond 1928), some is from anthropological reconstructions (Beals 1932, 1943, 1945), and some is reconstructed here on the basis of comparison of modern materials with historical sources, such as the accounts of early Spanish missionaries (Perez de Rivas 1944). The first period was characterized in all likelihood by a low population density, scattered rancheria settlement pattern, a band level of organization integrated through food and drink exchange, likely ceremonialized to some extent. Leadership was shamanistic, and the use of fetishes in family or resident kin group curing rites and rites of passage probably played a large part in maintaining band integration in times of peace. War as such was probably not an extensive activity. Whether the antecedents of the present Mayos lived in the river valley at this conjectural period of social development is a question to be determined by archaeological investigation. A corn origin myth alleges that the Mayos in the first age of time lived by gathering acorns, before corn was given to them. I leave that age to the archaeologists, for the period with which we begin is probably already characterized by corn horticulture.

The presence in Mayo society today of ceremonial and social exchange patterns between households in a small scale fiesta pattern, especially as regards curing by shamans, resembles in some rather particular details the beer-drinking and fiesta networks described by Kennedy (1963: 623-8) among the non-Christian Tarahumaras. Household ceremonies for death anniversaries, curing of children and crops by shaman, libations of sacred corn drink, and a variety of other resemblances between the two systems exist throughout Mayo history and persist in survivals today. A cult of sun, moon, and star deities, especially the morning star, probably dates from this time or earlier, as well as some of the other cults shared by the central Utoaztecans (Spicer 1964). The Tarahumaras are closely related linguistically and culturally to the Mayos and Yaquis and all the Cahitan speaking river and hill tribes or groups, but they have a less closely or complexly integrated social organization than the Cahitan river peoples.

Kennedy (1963: 632-5) accounts for the great degree of stability in level of social organization among the Tarahumaras in part by the effect of the corn-beer-drinking network itself. The scattered settlement pattern and removal from opportunity for contact with other groups, along with a large territory and the general lack of appeal of the available mestizo culture, are recognized as the base set of ecological factors. Though he feels that the beer exchange complex bleeds Tarahumara creativity, dissipates the corn surplus, and dominates such a large percentage of any given individual's time as to hinder culture growth, he also recognizes and emphasizes its euphoric roles.

The main point to be made here is that if a group possessing a socio-ceremonial integrative pattern and corn-based economy similar to that of the Tarahumaras, came into a rich alluvial valley, or if the pattern diffused to a group resident there, the population would probably grow rapidly and thus necessitate new means of social integration and eventually stimulate an emergent level of social organization. Any dissipative effects of the complex would be balanced off by its integrative effects in the more favorable environment. The canyons and irregular topography of the Tarahumara area prevent much interaction, or at least slow down social interaction considerably. In the river areas, on the other hand, travel is fairly easy up and down the waterways. Even though thorn forest slows traffic across the alluvial plain, it is an easier barrier across which to make trails. Land and water resources are correspondingly more favorable in the valley. Mayo pueblos and rancherías, as one would expect, were found by the first Spanish explorers primarily along the waterways, as they are today.

A second prehispanic period may have begun, as a sheer guess, not much earlier than 1000 A.D. and ended with the first Spanish contact. By this time Mayo society may well have reached a tribal level of integration. Near the end of the period, Spanish estimates put the Mayo population at 30,000. Even if this should be a high estimate, and it appears to be a careful count, the population density was comparatively great considering that the rancherías and settlements were concentrated in the lower twenty or thirty miles of the Mayo River banks and seasonal washes to the sides of it.

These settlements became larger and more closely spaced than Tarahumara rancherías. Corn, beans, and squash were raised. Fishing was a fairly large industry on the coast. Drying of fish rubbed with salt would have permitted the trade of this product inland. Much of the trading may have taken place between individuals meeting in a household fiesta complex. Some specialized hunting communities were located in the forest areas. Cotton clothing for agricultural peoples is described in early Spanish accounts, but the people in hunting villages wore clothes made of the animal skins that they traded for corn and other products. In other words, the roots of a regional economic specialization were forming and trade was developing, though no evidence of a highly secular market exists. Also, it appears that the Mayo organization was already composite, or at least cognatic and in the process of absorbing groups which at one time probably formed separate societies, or some of whom may have been refugee groups.

Leadership was still largely charismatic, although a council of heads of residential units existed near the end of the period with peace and war leaders and subsidiary officials (Spicer 1962: 372-84). This council appears to have presided over a pan-tribal initiation of warriors which could gather together several hundred to a thousand men at once in the Northern Mayo country by the time of first Spanish contacts. However, Mayo military sodalities also fought with a technique of using small hit and run groups. So a knowledge of a variety of war strategies appropriate to any of several particular kinds of occasion had developed or had been borrowed.

Chances are that some of this military strategy and organization had diffused with a cult or cults using bird and snake symbolisms, from the South, together with the idea of warrior-priesthoods, and which was adopted after the population density had created sufficient pressures to require these defense-offense arrangements. Some of the cults may have first entered the area through traders. These were then perhaps joined with the household fiesta exchange pattern, and the local functionaries corresponding to warrior-priests became honored and essential guests at these affairs, coming to have specific functions such as dancing and speech-making. Their dances, songs, forms of sculpture, and painting became ornaments of varieties of native shamanism. As late as 1910, members of the military society, called *wikicim* (birds), were known by a variety of ranks named for specific kinds of birds. Birds with topknots were of particularly high rank, along with parrots. As late as 1920, the feather worn by a warrior indicated his rank. Women were apparently formally trained in defense fighting, wore feathers, and went to battle. They met Spaniards in the 1500's and 1600's.

War was at this time a religious as well as practical activity, and it formed an important element in the total status system as well as in the world view of the Mayos. Like the birds and the other "animals of the claw," however, no Mayo killed except for a reason, which in his system was mostly defense of land, health, or family. Land competition made a standing army necessary.

Other members of the present military society, or of a division of it, are also known in certain contexts by animal names. Specifically the *go'im*, or coyotes, function today as policemen during certain fiestas. Formerly a go'i (coyote), danced in the ceremonial ramada at fiestas, as did a wikit (bird dancer), the paskola, and deer dancer. The Mayo classification of clawed animals together with birds is justified mythologically by their common origin. The paskola seems to be like a shaman priest to what was at one time a rain cult involved with snake symbolism. He is today called the priest of the cult of the Huya'Ania, or forest world of the invisible animals. Obviously, however, simple control over the animals as such was not the object of any of the cults, but the arrangements between the holy animals and between men were conceived to be included in some kind of total relationship which had to be understood and perpetuated in terms of cult activities. Mating, feasting, and war of the animals were related to the same activities of human groups.

The earlier cults of the sun and moon and stars were tied in with the rain cult, which drew on the natural phenomena of clouds and concepts of visible and invisible rain water in pools and the responsiveness of the earth life to such water. If people were sick, curing involved all these kinds of relationships. The maintenance of life, health, and abundance was conceived to be related to all the corresponding animals who symbolized the processes of nature, because these relations involved human affairs and vice versa.

This is a key to the understanding of Mayo sodality structures and perhaps of tribal social and cultural integrations in general. Such integrations arose in concert with a world view of total survival, related to curing and rites of passage, perpetuating the general balance of nature through birth, infancy, maturity, love, and death, including human conflict as an aspect of this. This is why war was an orientation at this stage of Mayo development. The character of the meaning system, as well as the social structures of the sodalities, was subsequently much modified through the mission period, so that meanings and forms became far less explicit in the Mayos' statements about this kind of world view. Human archetypes in the forms of the saints assumed a greater relative importance than animal and metamorphosic archetypes, though there were already many human gods in the prehispanic pantheon.

Inevitably the question arises, however, as to whether these sodalities and others like them first developed within any systematic connection with localized or dispersed kinship groups. Any detailed or complex proposal awaits a detailed comparative study of kinship in Cahitan and Northwest Mexican Utoaztecan groups. Nevertheless it appears that the composite nature of Mayo kinship was earlier some cognatic form which enabled it to absorb outside individuals or groups readily into its organization. Absorption of enemies by keeping of captive women is probably a very early pattern. The terms indicate bilateral

organization. Ranchería exogamy is an ancient pattern. Similarly, in reconstructing Yaqui culture of about 1600, Spicer (1961: 14) notes that present terminology would indicate ranchería exogamy, absence of lineages, bilateral extended family as the basic social units. He adds, "Precisely what the character and strength of kinship ties were we do not know. The immediate acceptance of the Spanish program of 'reduction' and the evidences of tribe-wide military organization point to the interpretation that segmentation on a kinship basis was not strongly developed."

Moiety-like divisions in ceremonial organization today have no known marriage prescription but appear to be purely ceremonial in function, as among some Eastern Pueblos of the Southwest United States.

Spanish Contact Period, 1533-1771

Warfare and intergroup competition during this period is characterized in its earliest phases by clashes with small Spanish groups allied with Yaquis. A mining exploration group skirted the Mayo country in the 1560's because they said the Mayos were restless and hungry due to a recent devastating flood (Hammond and Rey 1928). At about the same time a Franciscan mission, San Juan de Carapoa, was reported to have been set up on the Fuerte River, immediately to the South of the Mayos. It was short-lived due to the hostility of the indigenous people there and lack of Crown support for the mission. However the mission may well have played some part in the receptive attitudes the Mayos subsequently showed in requesting missionaries in 1601, and in forming military alliance with the Spaniards in 1609, and finally in receiving Jesuit missionaries in 1614.

Following the arrival of the Jesuits, intergroup relations were characterized by a long period of peace lasting over a century until 1740. During this period a tight and effective intersocietal and intercultural cooperation was formed with the Jesuit organization. In that year the peaceful relationship of the missionaries and the Mayos reached a turning point. A large rebellion occurred in which Mayos drove out non-Mayos from Mayo country below Navojoa. The disaster of 1740 appears to have culminated as a consequence of growing discontent with economic exploitation of Mayo individuals and resources, which began with the opening of mines and haciendas in Mayo country in the 1680's. This exploitation, which steadily gained in intensity, as well as dissatisfaction with some abuses of the mission government system, appear to have been at the root of the rebellion.

Population and settlement patterns underwent some drastic changes between 1533 and 1771. Immediately following missionization, a rapid and substantial reduction is indicated in available censuses. These reflect in part the emigration of Mayos to do wage labor in mines and haciendas. In the beginning of this period some 30,000 Mayos occupied the lower part of the river from Alamos Mountain south. Disease also took a heavy toll in the Mayo area. The demographic picture shows drastic changes within a very short time after the beginning of the mission period. By the beginning of the next period in 1771 only 6,000 Mayos were living in villages. The Indian system of landholding remained little changed however. Though some changes occurred in the social organization of village management due to the acceptance of the system of governors, annually elected with their assistants, land was still owned in a combined system of communal lands within which individual rights emerged. Toward the end of the 1600's Spanish haciendas began to move into the land left vacant by the reduction of Mayo population.

The main economic pattern of Mayo life in the villages continued basically unchanged, with additions of new plants, animals, and tools. Granaries were associated with churches, and distribution through a fiesta economy remained very important, though it shifted in part to church centers.

The most significant changes of the period were in town organization, leadership, the founding of the church organization and the linking of old sodalities to it with much remodification. What were probably entirely new sodalities were founded in the process. And the tying in of what were military societies into the religious system — as Spicer points out (1954b: 673) — was likely "an elaboration and intensification of an already existing close linkage." These changes took place during a period of peace and must be understood to be connected with missionization as the dominant condition of contact rather than other kinds of intergroup relations, such as warfare, or other types of environmental changes. In fact, after the mission period, if not earlier, the most significant environmental changes for Mayos were in the form of contact relationships and related organizational changes.

In religious structure there were also reorganizations in the pantheon, perhaps less with respect to "meanings and functions" than to "names and forms" (Spicer 1954b: 672), as well as in ritual, myth, and some social organizations. Church-to-church ceremonial exchange was encouraged by the missionaries (Ross and Lynne Crumrine, fieldnotes). House-to-house ceremonial exchange very probably persisted and may have well been strengthened in the long period of peace and relative prosperity between 1614 and 1740.

The transition from this period to the next began in the open conflict of 1740 and ended in 1771. The Jesuits were expelled in 1767. Secularization of the missions was attempted in 1771, coinciding with the growth of power of local Spanish interests seeking to break up Mayo landholding units and exploit Mayo labor. Mayos were asked to pay taxes for the first time in 1772. All of this followed a large flood in 1770 which had laid the group open to hunger, disease, and social disorganization. The cultural ecology of the Mayos had become gradually transformed from a situation of intercultural cooperation to a new era characterized by intergroup hostility with non-Mayos. Because of the anomalous character of infiltrating settlers, they were much more difficult to mass against than other Indian groups which were clearly identifiable as organized enemies. The Spanish settlers were a heterogeneous group, lacking unity, yet were not amenable to absorption in Mayo society. They took up the land vacated by the depopulation of the Mayos. The mission system, which had served to protect Mayos from taxation and excessive labor and land exploitation, had lost its position of power in the Spanish empire.

The Autonomous Period, 1771-1887

Marking the beginning of the Autonomous Period, the attempts of the secular clergy to enter and take control of the Mayo churches were largely a failure, as were the attempts to exact taxes. Mayos were too strong in their own territory to be subjected to religious or economic control during this period. In a sense, however, because Mayos entered into wage labor and left their farm lands, many inroads were made into Mayo economic independence which accomplished what legal and military means could not.

Intergroup competition was apparent throughout this period, and it flared into open and bitter fighting in the 1820's, 1860's, 1870's, and 1880's. Mayos call this era their hundred years of war. Strong rival leadership was developing in the Sonoran mestizo state organization, and Mayos were used, as were Yaquis, by mestizo caudillos warring for power against one another. Toward the end of the 1870's, pan-Indian federations against Mexicans developed impressive strengths. Mayo surrender marks the end of the period.

Early in the period the demographic situation showed vast changes, with only 6,000 Mayos in the mission communities. Thousands of other Mayos were living on haciendas and in mining communities in and near the independent Mayo settlements, however, and apparently maintained family ties and contacts there. Some took refuge in other Cahitan communities. Such refugee communities were perhaps a mechanism for the pan-Cahitan spirit beginning to develop. Numbers of mestizos in the Mayo territory increased steadily throughout this period until by the middle of the 1800's the northern part of the country was firmly controlled by mestizo hacendados. Mayo organization still posed a tremendous military threat at this time below Navojoa and periodically Mayos drove out foreign, or non-Mayo, settlers from the down-river area.

During this period the economic pattern that had long characterized Mayo society remained largely intact. Independent fishing, agricultural, and forest villages remained side by side with the growing intrusive haciendas. The haciendas did not pose the same kind of threat that the more urban mining centers and rail centers of later periods in the northern Mayo country came to have. Legal measures to break up landholding systems which preserved Mayo solidarity continued to be enacted during this period, in 1828-29, but still with little or no results.

The pre-Christian tribal organization had been permanently modified during the Mission Period, but during the Autonomous Period society and culture took much of its lasting power from the solidarity created through church organization which brought unity between the cults of the military sodalities, the lay priesthood organization, and church sodalities which had developed during the earlier period. The

military sodalities had survived through the long peace of the mission period, largely perhaps, as a result of fulfilling ceremonial and religious functions. Lay ministers, probably formerly connected with a cult of the sun, came to fulfill many of the functions of the former missionary priest as well as other functions that were aboriginal in character. The ministers established a close working relationship with military and jural leadership. These were in turn also much influenced by the Spanish system, and with shamans of native prehispanic cults, a variety of which survived with little apparent change throughout the mission period.

During the Autonomous Period, when the unsteady peace with the hacendados erupted from time to time into open and extended conflict, the council system of the Mayo church cult leaders, governors, shamans, and elders showed itself to be a relatively smoothly working organization. Coinciding with the end of Spanish control, federation of Mayos with other Indian groups evidenced considerable advance over earlier periods.

The Autonomous Period was characterized mainly by an increase in Mayo solidarity and refinement of Cahitan-Spanish fused social organization. Growing competition culminating in thirty years of conflict against non-Indians, rather than other Indian groups, stands out as one of the most important features of the intercultural environment. Until the end of the period Mayos staved off the attempts of the intrusive groups to break up their land and to subjugate them politically. Yet through surrender and withdrawal in 1887 they removed themselves from the conflict when the price of victory seemed suicide. Even at this date, the idea of full and permanent submission was evidently difficult to accept.

Mayo military power was almost totally crippled, certainly until the rise of a new generation. The arrangements made by the state for the return of the Mayos to their land on surrendering did enable what was left of families to regroup on farm lands within the limits of what had been their tribal territories. The state legislature, however, passed a law enabling a development company in 1890 to open up a canal between Camoa and Navojoa. They were allowed (1) to take up to two-thirds of the river water, (2) to condemn lands for right of way for the main canal, for other canals, and for necessary maintenance roads, and (3) any other materials deemed necessary to execute this project. Only a few days notice was given to any previous owners (Doubdab 1964: 406-7).

Colonization of the Mayo area by non-Mayos began with the consistent and planned backing of a state and national state government which would never again allow a period of relatively peaceful autonomy to Mayos. Change would be directed affecting some aspect or another of Mayo life through economic or political controls of the dominant state. The intercultural ecology was to be characterized thenceforth by a steady relative increase of non-Mayos in numbers, and in their political, economic, and military power. A steady non-Mayo encroachment upon Mayo land and resources was accompanied by direct suppression of Mayo religious and military organization and in imposition of direct economic controls.

The Relocation Period, 1887-1961

The Relocation Period can be divided into three main parts, the first of which ends in 1910. Mayos call the period in which Porfirio Diaz was President, the Porfiriata. It is a convenient term by which to designate a period mainly characterized by a hostile peace, at the cost of total subjugation by hacendado and state police. It was a time characterized by the rapid increase in Mayo country of non-Mayo population, the drawing of numbers of Mayos into hacienda peonage, the systematic killing and deportation of Mayo leaders and their families. There were attempts on the part of local hacendados to prevent tribal gatherings of any type and to destroy the native councils and political organizations. Independent economic life was maintained by only a few Mayos in remote areas. Nevertheless the fiesta exchange system must have been maintained to some extent. But the survival of any sense of Mayo identity and social organization probably depended on two processes. One was the symbolic value of considering the hacendados enemies. The other was in maintaining this nucleus of independent communities which carried on the cult rituals and provided symbols of the Mayo way of life to those Mayos who were in peonage or who had been deported to other parts of Mexico.

Early in this period Mayo religious action developed into a movement of sufficient scope to cause

serious concern to Mexican officials. This was probably in part in direct response to the canal contract mentioned previously. The symbolism of the movement involved magical nativism in a form so intense that Mexican military men watched with considerable trepidation as all the Mayos left their work in haciendas and mines and mills and gathered by thousands in a half dozen places in the northern Mayo country to hear their prophets speak of the coming of the end of the world, which was to take place by flood. The reinstitution of Mayo politico-religious organization as an object of some of the rituals is indirectly indicated (Troncoso 1905), as in the placing of bows upon altars, along with flowers, as described by one Mexican spy who had been sent in to see what was going on. Mexicans further suspected war plans when one of the prophets turned out to be related to a former Mayo military leader.

Just to be safe, the Mexican generals ordered the prophets, who numbered some seven in all, plus some other leaders and most of their families, to be gathered up and deported to work in a mine in Lower California. Mayos then attacked Navojoa with bows and arrows in 1892 under Totoriwoki and another Mayo war leader who had been spared in the earlier roundup. Their object was to get supplies to continue the resistance. They were quickly put down.

As effective as these methods were in temporarily squelching Mayo power, they provided martyrs for the Mayo people which would serve as a symbolic nucleus for reconsolidation of Mayo organization during and after the Mexican Revolution of 1910.

A regular colonization program for non-Mayo settlers in the Mayo country was set up. Legal measures to break up commonly held forest lands were instituted. For the first time such measures met with some success because of the increasing military and police power of the non-Mayos and the breakdown of Mayo military strength. In order to maintain power over Mayos, local hacendados instituted measures repressive to religious activity in general, using the anti-church laws of the Constitution of 1857, which had been intended for other purposes.

The second major division of the present period began with the Revolution of 1910. The cultural and physical ecological changes brought by this period of chaotic conflict were enormous. The years between 1914 and 1921 were characterized by particular upheaval in Mayo country. The most salient feature of change was an abortive attempt to turn the relationship with large landholders upside down (Obregon 1950; Gill 1957). Some Mayos took the opportunity to avenge themselves for injustices at the hands of particular hacendados and Mexicans. In the earliest stages of the wars some went out as Mayo military units under Mexican commanders. Later Mayos fought in groups of one or two thousand under Mayo command. At least for brief periods they fought in terms of Mayo interests and orientations. Later they formed alliances with and were placed under command of Mexican generals. Some units were broken up as they went north. They thought what Madero offered was a return of the government to the people, and conceived of this as the reinstitution of the full autonomy of Mayo pueblo governments. In return for their participation on behalf of the various Mexican caudillos, particularly Carranza, they were offered many promises, one of which was a return of Mayo lands. At various times Mayos fought with Villa, Carranza, Obregon, and independently under Mayo leadership. Many times families were divided against one another, unaware they were on different sides, so confused was this period. Mayos, internally divided as were Yaquis (Spicer 1945), fought on one side or another in every major battle of this period.

In 1914 a large flood accentuated the developing crisis, bringing economic distress and disease. With the movement of the main battles of the war to the north in 1915 the Mayo country was ravaged. Mayo population was decimated by the fighting both through death and emigration to escape the plundering. Mestizos and non-Mayos moved into the vacuum. As the war subsided temporarily many Mayos returned to the Mayo country to find their families had all been killed or had fled; often some stranger was occupying their lands. The power of the hacendados and their private police systems was greater and more ruthlessly used than ever.

Religious suppression continued into 1931 and later. In 1926 local Mexicans were hired by hacendados to burn the local Mayo churches and saints' images. Navojoa church was spared, as was that of Camalobo, ironically because they had local priests. Mayos interpret this action, not as an anti-clerical move, under which law it was justified by the Mexicans, but as revenge for the damage they as Mayos had inflicted on these particular Mexicans in the earlier battles, and on the Mexican centers they had raided and burned during the Revolution.

For ten years the Bánari church was not rebuilt, nor were those in many of the other Indian villages where religious life had to all intents and purposes been completely suppressed. Mayo religious life in the surviving churches was closely watched for signs of rebellion or organization on the part of the Mayos. Dr. Ralph Beals (1943: 90-1) visited the Mayos of Navojoa during this period in 1930 to 1932 and came away with the feeling that Mayo religion was essentially dead.

If we can infer anything from subsequent events, however, Mayos were at pains to show no evidence of inner feelings that might betray their wish to reorganize their independent and autonomous pueblo church units. They spoke quietly for fear of deportation, death, or brutality to their families, which they had seen repeatedly during the last generation. The richness and compelling quality of the present Mayo mythology which refers to the decade of 1926-1936 shows that Mayo religious emotions were indeed stirred, especially because of the burning of the saints' images and of the churches. These were grouped symbolically with the earlier prophets and pueblo officials who had been deported in the 1890's, with their families and small children, to the mine in the west, known now among Mayos as Los Mártiros.

In 1931 there were small uprisings in Huatabampo and in Etchojoa aimed specifically at certain Mexican officials. The enemy was no longer all the mestizos, for the Mayos had found common causes with some of the poorer mestizos and some of the kinder hacendados, with whom they were willing to make peace. They now aimed their attacks at *specific* officials, hacendados, and lawyers who were particularly oppressive in their actions and aims. This change in conflict orientation may be viewed as an adaptation to an intercultural ecology which now included perhaps as many non-Mayos in the area as Mayos, the vast majority of whom lived in the same, or greater, poverty than the Mayos. To hope to drive all these people out was no longer militarily realistic. Mayos had even become symbolically united with them in terms of the ideas of the doctrines of Madero and Zapata. They aimed at the head of the organization in each pueblo and depended on an Act of God to do the rest.

The third division of the present period begins in 1936 and lasts to the present. Throughout this period an unsteady peace brought Mexican troops into the area from time to time. Some road and rail networks destroyed during the period of conflict were restored and substantially enlarged. Schools were restored and enlarged. New schools and medical facilities were provided in most pueblos of any size at all. Appointed officials of the municipality state system resided in every pueblo. A state militia was on call from major towns of the area and was occasionally called out when there were rumors of Mayo uprisings. Electricity and piped water reached villages miles from urban centers. All these features of Mexican technology and political organization were available to Mayos, though they were appreciated only to a limited degree in some communities. Economic control through government bank financing and water control was inescapable for all ejidatarios, however, whether Mayo or not. Through the forcing of Mayos to plant cash crops, pay for river water from the irrigation systems, pay taxes on roads and canals, and through other economic sanctions, a steady force for directed change has proceeded throughout this period from the national state, affecting mainly the economic system, but indirectly influencing other aspects of culture.

Mayos numbered 15,000 early in the period. But the population rapidly increased as Mayos returned from all parts of Mexico after the long periods of war. This immigration, together with the general effects of a population explosion in Sonora, where the rate of births over deaths was higher than in Mexico generally, makes sensible the estimate of 40,000 individuals identifying themselves as Mayos. The figure is probably reasonable despite the intensive assimilation of numbers of Mayos into the mestizo society during this period. However, non-Mayos probably still outnumbered Mayos three to one in their own former territory. This population was also growing rapidly.

A new impersonal wage-labor pattern had replaced hacienda peonage. A free market economy and a free labor market were strong and exerting considerable influence on Mayos. The fiesta distribution system, however, appeared to be stimulated by the relative availability of money. The increased regrouping and solidarity of Mayo families permitted by a relative increase of land occupation as compared with the period of the haciendas, together with the reforming of church and pueblo centers with the relative lifting of steady religious suppression, made this possible. However, though farmlands were gained, common village thorn forest and grazing lands continued to be diminished. In accordance with a national plan, this rich land was to be opened up and farmed to help feed Mexico's hungry millions. But the loss of this land to Mayos caused a crisis, especially to town-dwellers, because of diminishing sources of fuel and housebuilding materials without a concomitant increase in wages to cover this loss. The pace of population growth far exceeded establishment of ejidos as the Ejido Period proceeded. A large number of young Mayos were landless and without preparation for alternative occupations. In years when the crops of large landowners of the area failed and farm wage work was scarce, there was economic crisis.

Nevertheless, with the founding of ejidos and the giving of deeds to the Mayos who had hung onto their small plots of land through the conflict and suffering of previous periods, the excess cultural energy of the Mayos went into reestablishment of the burned churches and re-creation of their social organizations. Pueblo and church councils were reinstituted or came out in the open. Though the ejidos also have councils as provided for in the national organization, and the pueblos have Mexican and Mayo officials existing side by side, these Mayo organizations continued to spring up in similar form to the pre-1890 period. Furthermore, ceremonial exchange between them developed through the reinstitution of old exchanges that were felt to have been traditional and also through new exchanges instituted by prophets with personal patron saints, and through household cults.

Two such movements are reported in 1945 and 1957 (Erasmus 1952, 1961). Both movements tried to change the forms of both Mayo and mestizo government. Specifically they attempted to expand and strengthen Autonomous Period forms of Mayo local government and religious hierarchy and to replace the mestizo officials with Mayo ones. Supernatural and magical elements dominated these movements, however. So far they have resulted mainly in changing the Mayo religious system. The second movement was based particularly closely on the general pattern of the Mayo religious nativism of the 1890's. But in the movements of 1945 and 1957 the means of control immediately applied by the state governments on the cult leaders differed from earlier techniques. The travel of cult leaders was restricted; they were paid cash in amounts of what were to the poor Mayos large sums, as inducements to curtail religious activities. Officials of other tribes, particularly the Yaqui governors, were encouraged to consider the movement dangerous to their own interests and prevent its spread into Yaqui country by officially discouraging and intimidating the Mayo leadership. In short it appears that the power and authority of the state organization, as well as the sophistication of its methods, had reached such a level that it could successfully inhibit some significant developments in Indian organization.

Unless unforeseen changes are made, however, it cannot assimilate the Mayo organization entirely, given the present situation in which Mayos are alienated by dissatisfaction with their highly unequal economic and political participation in the state organization, and therefore considering themselves remaining outside that organization. On the national level in Mexico there appears to be some interest in incorporating tribal organizations as such. This has not been local policy in Sonora, however, and national practices have often had the opposite effect.

PERSISTENCE AND CHANGE

Throughout the periods of Mayo development which we have traced here we can see that sodality organization has persisted from the second prehispanic period. Tribal-wide initiations of young men into warrior sodalities continued. In periods of peace such an organization served the church cults in a ceremonial capacity under command of church-pueblo officials. This adaptation may be one of the most important mechanisms enabling Mayos to survive as a people into the present period.

The gradual transformation of Mayo economy from a subsistence farming, fishing, hunting equilibrium to a small nucleus of independent farmers heavily dependent on wage labor appears to be a fundamental transformation in ecological relationships. But it is perhaps most significant that the fiesta distribution system connected with religious organization has persisted. This is the segment of the economy to which the particular and distinctive forms of Mayo group life are most closely related. The labor is a more important element than the production of goods involved in the exchange. Let us examine these ideas.

A very strong ideal pattern among Mayos is that religious life should be based on a primary resource-oriented economy. Only a few specialists are exempt from cultivating a subsistence plot. Almost all Mayo families farm tiny plots and do wage labor to meet the cash needs, mostly for clothes. Maestro, maestro mo'oro, and a few other high officials are "clothed" by the fiesteros — that is, the things for which they need cash are bought for them, which frees them from the necessity for performing wage labor. In addition, a plot for the church is farmed, the proceeds being given to a church treasury to be used for repairs and necessary grooming before the great fiestas. Such a production system directly generates the food for distribution. The fact is, however, that production has changed drastically. This is because of the requirement that crops be geared to the national export-import system. The national ejido bank, which finances ejido crops, requires this. At least five out of six Mayo plots of ejidatarios in Bánari church in 1961 were planted in cotton, oil grains, or wheat — all cash crops — not at all useful for direct exchange in Mayo ceremonial networks — but not altogether from Mayo choice. In the vast majority of cases the only financing obtainable for water and seed was through the ejidal bank; the Mayos were thus forced to plant their parcels of land or risk losing membership in the ejido. Directed change in terms of economic sanctions from the national level has, in this way, exerted considerable indirect effect on the religious system.

It is still true, however, that control of corn production spells power within Mayo society. A handful of the most influential Mayos supplied corn from their own fields for important rituals of the yearly round. Some of these individuals have remained in the authority structure for long periods, and some of their lands are used by other poorer Mayos without charge.

Mayo ideal patterns of fiesta-giving involve raising the food, preparing it with one's own labor, and giving it, not selling it, in a ceremonial context. These elements are repeatedly spoken of when it is necessary for Mayos to explain deviations from this ideal from time to time. The bread rosaries referred to in the section on ceremonial exchange described above serve as an example. Mayo women supplying them to the fiesteros are supposed to bake them at home in earth ovens. One woman who had bought the loaves at a bakery was much gossiped about, but her rosary was used and apparently worked for its purpose as well as any other. Formerly bannari, atole made for the termination of the Santa Kurus fiesta at Homecarit, was made by the fiestero family from its own orn. Fiesteros were heard complaining about the xpense of buying the large supply of corn necessary o make the drink — that it was a great hardship to et the cash all at once. Thus one may now buy the orn, or even the flour, but the labor of making the lrink or the rosary is still required. The labor involved in the fiesta, the marching, food preparation, itual labor, cannot be bought for cash, even though people recognize that the food must now be bought in some cases rather than prepared from home-grown produce.

Continual essential compromises are being made as ar as the production system is concerned. Even the oods of exchange to some extent have been adaptable to change. Wheat bread is used for bread rosaries and even for feeding the masked soldiers of Pilate at he end of Holy Week, a ritual act likely derived hrough many stages of change long forgotten by Mayos today from what was once a corn ritual. Mescal was probably substituted in many contexts for a corn beer like Tarahumara *sugui*.

But you cannot eat cotton. Mayos often made such a statement in 1961, recognizing explicitly the changes forced upon them in religious-economic integration. The next best alternative, in order to preserve the rest of the religious system, was to buy corn. Since much of it was imported from Iowa, according to informants, it was very expensive. Though the importance of food production has necessarily diminished in actuality, the emphasis on distribution continues. After all it is the next link in the maintenance of the religious and economic integration.

The gradual change in the land-holding systems of the Mayos during the Porfiriata had to some extent been effective in changing Mayo life, but the ejidos and the other protective measures, taken as a result of the Revolution of 1910 to insure a land base for the Indians, provide today almost as effective a land base as the original system did in some respects, except that there is not enough of such land to go around. Mayo ejidos are today of both the communal type, in which all profits are shared and land is used in common, and of the parceled type in which individuals within the ejido farm plots of their own, though these cannot be legally inherited from parent to child. This disturbs the ancestor-oriented Mayos.

What Mayos consider their village forests were still being continually cut and transformed into farmland by latifundistas in 1961, and in some areas in the northern part of the Mayo country an occasional ejido is founded. But no ejidos had been granted in the Huatabampo municipality for some time prior to 1961. Most of the ejidos there were formed on land expropriated from foreign holdings in the late 1930's and 1940's. Mayos and poor mestizos were sharply aware of this fact. In 1963 the Law of Colonization was ended.

Adding to land scarcity as a feature of present ecology, the population picture shows a greater number of Mayos existing today than ever before in history. In 1760 there were no more than 6,000 Mayos left from the original 30,000. After 1760 the Mayo population remained below a level proportionate to its ecological niche, creating a vacuum into which non-Mayos rushed. Even as late as 1940 there were only some 15,000 Mayos in the river municipalities along with some 70,000 non-Mayos (Estado de Sonora 1957). In the subsequent twenty years both populations roughly doubled. Irrigation and mechanized farm technology had begun as early as the 1890's, and by the 1940's characterized the majority of farms in the region. In 1961 the area remained primarily agricultural in terms of total economy — mestizo and Mayo — with only a few very small scale canning and mechanical industries in the towns.

As for the other aspects of Mayo social organization, in addition to the persistence of sodalities, the native church cults and officials continued in much the same pattern of organization during the Autonomous Period, with church-pueblo councils incorporating the entire list of officials and sodality heads. Only the elders were weakened. The civil governors had become fused with the church governors, though there were ten, the original number of governors. Shamanistic leadership was much like that of prehispanic periods in some respects, though the leaders exerted power used to unite groups across pueblo lines, often in league with the church official organizations. Magical nativism stimulated the development of new ceremonial exchange networks. These networks integrated pueblos which had formerly segmented by fission into new pueblo-church cults. Multification of pueblo cults provided increased opportunity for participation in religious activities by the growing Mayo population. Symbolic complementarity of saints provided the rationale for consolidation.

Mayo identity was re-enforced by the existence of a social organization and cultural belief system still integrated in an underlying structure which was North American Indian in type. A Mayo who visited ceremonies in a United States Western pueblo alleged, "Those people are not baptised as we are, but they are yoremem [Mayo word for themselves, also generalized here to other Indians]." What led him to say this was a recognition of a type of pueblo life encompassing a spiritual relationship with nature. This involved a concept of the supernaturals as the harmonizing element between all areas, divisions, seasons of nature and the earth's productivity, with the stages of human life, the divisions of human social organization, and with the use of human labor in harvesting and donating surplus food and drink as a means of perpetuating this harmony. The part played by sodality structures and authority of shaman-priesthood in this system confirms the social link which he perceived.

Mayos are somewhat assimilated in all aspects of life, except in those that relate to the type of religious system described. They think of themselves as loyal Mexicans as well as Mayos. Nevertheless they still form a society separate from and opposed to the local Mexican Catholic churches and the local mestizo communities.

Their religious beliefs are in clear contrast to the Mexican Catholic ethic of individual salvation and eternal rewards and punishments after death (Spicer 1964) and conflict with some, though not all, of the basic values associated with the economic entrepreneurial system. Productivity and accumulation are encouraged to a point, provided that distribution takes place within the religious fiesta system. Ownership of house and farm lands by individuals is accepted but does not conflict strongly in this respect with earlier ideas. Pueblo ownership of common lands is still a strongly held idea and is ritually recognized in many religious ceremonies. Land is not yet, however, a commodity to be freely bought and sold, a cultural fact recognized in ejido policy.

Of all aspects of economic-religious integration, the emphasis upon labor, as a function of both economic and ritual fiesta activities, is the most important aspect of the system and the aspect in which least departure from ideal patterns is tolerated. Work, though it has become a commodity on the intercultural economic scene with the increasing importance of wage labor, is not a commodity in the fiesta system. It cannot be bought and sold. Its sacredness relative to the decrease in sacredness of food production is a salient fact of Mayo cultural structure (as it is for Yaquis, Spicer 1954a).

In the face of such thoroughgoing changes, the interdependency relations between tribal organization, the ceremonial exchange of pan-tribal sodalities, the fiesta economy with an emphasis on donation of time and individual labor as well as goods, and the complementarity of localized supernaturals, all are relationships which are solid and ancient, even though the exterior form and details would make the organization unrecognizable to precontact-age Mayos were they to see it today.

RELATION OF CHANGING ECOLOGICAL FACTORS TO FEATURES OF MAYO SOCIAL ORGANIZATION

Ecological changes through time directly relating to features of the present level of Mayo social organization may be grouped under several main headings in combination: (1) influences of topographic features, (2) factors of intergroup competition, (3) demographic and geographic features, and (4) economic arrangements.

Topographic

In early periods the variety of forest zones, and the river, coastal, and mountain habitats, permitted the rapid growth of a late-level tribal organization because of the food variety and abundance they provided and the external and internal trade made possible by ports and rivers.

One other important feature of Mayo ecology, indeed of all the river peoples who lived in the lower plains, was the importance of the flood, both as an irrigating and fertilizing agent and, in its more rampant phases, as an agent of destruction of communities and fields, and as a bringer of suffering and disease. As mentioned earlier, Spanish mining records indicate that explorers skirted the Mayos because a flood in the mid-1500's had left many homeless and hungry on the Mayo River. The regularity of floods on the Mayo River, almost every forty to eighty years in recorded time, would provide an ecological imperative for the development of institutionalized social mechanisms. Agreements as to refuge areas and means for redistributing boundaries after the flood in case of changed river channels would seem essential. The flood idea also provided a nucleus for the gathering of supernatural symbols, from every available source. A rain mythology from the south diffused into the area preceding Christianity. With the coming of Christianity the Noah myth fused with earlier stories of the re-creation of the world after its destruction by flood.

It is conceivable that a chiefdom level of organization could well have arisen in such an environment, especially given continued competition from neighbors of the Mayos, but Spanish contact brought a definite close to this era by enforcing peace.

Intergroup Competition

In early periods Mayo tribal organization arose through competition and conflict with neighboring tribes and small chiefdoms. The mission period was not characterized at any time in the first part of the period by armed conflict with the Spanish. There was no full scale Mayo-Spanish warfare until the Spanish economic interest shifted from mining in the mountains on the edge of Mayo territory, to farming. This shift began to stimulate growth in mestizo settlements in the heart of the valley, coming into direct competition with Mayos. In 1740 the first Mayo-mestizo competition broke into open conflict, as has been noted. Mayo tribal organization was effective in competition with mestizo organizations, including chiefdom-like organizations associated with a frontier state, until 1890. At that time it became inadequate. Together with increasing military power, the frontier state which was in competition with Mayo tribal organization received support from the national state for setting up a colonization program in connection with a systematic canal irrigation system on the Mayo river. Mayo-mestizo demographic ratios changed steadily. Mayo hostility shifted to selected non-Mayos.

The military aspect of Mayo tribal organization had persisted with some variations over 350 years of contact; it was essentially crushed for the first time in 1890, and the leadership was deported and exiled.

But this military structure associated with the tribal organization emerged again during the Revolution of 1910 when social aspects of the ecological situation appeared to require a positively institutionalized aggressive response on the part of Mayo society.

Today the survival of tribal organization through ceremonial exchange, including groups derived from military sodalities, may be regarded less in terms of inter-ethnic competition and readiness for military defense than as a means of enculturation and maintenance of internal political organization and internal order. The primary manifest functions of such sodalities are to serve the saints' cults, to help teach the Mayo way of life to the members, and to maintain order within Mayo society itself. The maintenance of Mayo church-pueblo centers, distinct from mestizo urban market centers, is to be understood today less in terms of Mayo-mestizo hostility than in terms of the maintenance of the traditional Mayo sentiment system; a status-role system maintaining values that allow Mayos to feel worthwhile as human beings. The present tribe-like organization, then, from an offense-defense viewpoint, is a survival from the pre-1890 Mayo-mestizo conflict and the pre-1614 inter-Indian conflict. It was still more or less adaptive in the Revolution of 1910.

The extraordinary persistence of the internal organization of Mayo leadership and authority patterns relate to the ready adaptability of the pueblo-tribal type of organization to so many kinds of needs — defense, religious, political, economic, and internal social integration of units. Before and after the military power of the organization was subdued by 1890 and repeatedly threatened at later periods (1926, 1931) a high degree of religious fervor characterized the Mayo system as it does today. The magical quality of Mayo nativism may be more apparent than real, however, since it is always directed to, and sometimes results in strengthening, pan-tribal sodalities and intercommunity ties of many varieties, as well as to explicit control by Mayos of local elections, officials, and churches. It does not always succeed. Nevertheless it is an essentially rational, political, and peaceful adaptation, rather than a military one, to the intergroup competition of present ecological relationships.

Demographic

Several important categories of ecological variables impinge on Mayo demography: (1) natural variables such as floods and tropical storms; (2) disease and warfare and other variables connected with direct human agents; (3) availability of food and economic adaptation; (4) demographic characteristics, e.g. male-female ratios; and (5) the relative specificity or generality of ecological adaptation of competing populations once they complete an invasion and establish themselves in the social-cultural structure of contact (Kaplan 1960: 75). Features of the present tribal organization which appear to be responses to floods, epidemics, and the like are agreements as to flood refuge areas and procedures and, in part, composite household organization. Such demographic changes as were induced by natural catastrophes have been rather continuously coped with by Mayos through all periods, though disease and flood, for example, were especially effective in causing general distress by the late 1700's, adding to the cumulative effects of slave-raiding and emigration.

The present demographic situation of the area is characterized by a great increase of Mayos over all previous historic periods, but a far greater relative increase of non-Mayo neighbors, especially since 1890, who are involved in a more general form of economic adaptation than Mayos. In this way non-Mayos have been able to outgrow Mayos since 1890, in an ecological niche to which Mayos have been nevertheless previously more specifically adapted. The maintenance of Mayo tribal organization and the associated economic independence of primary segments in this demographic context is obviously no longer adaptive to the extent that the tribal organization interferes with a more general economic adaptation.

In connection with the population increase within Mayo society itself, however, the tribal organization has undergone some adaptive changes. In early periods rancherías characterized the Mayo settlement pattern. With the increase in population, rancherías became larger, more numerous, and closer to each other. The change from ranchería to church-centered pueblos in the mission period harmonized with the direction in which Mayo demographic-settlement patterns were moving. These persist today side by side with a more urban style of mestizo town (Spicer 1961: 71-2). However, the larger towns are also bordered at the edges by Mayo barrios, or districts. The fission of Mayo church-pueblo units into smaller units permits the maintenance of a ratio of churches to Mayo population at between 1:2500 and 1:3000. The pattern of church cult and pueblo fission is thus adaptive to the maintenance of the Mayo enculturation system. The question of whether a larger population is an adaptation or not can of course be argued.

Economic

Economic aspects of tribal organization, including the emphasis on primary resources such as food and physical labor, show important evidence of continuities from prehistoric times, and though a great deal of modification has taken place in Mayo economy, these emphases persisted through the Spanish period and into the Mexican periods. Hacienda and later free farm labor did not fundamentally change the Mayo values for these aspects of the economy, though these work patterns broke into Mayo economic autonomy. Work on the land, however, was still fundamental, whereas mining, for example, in the Alamos area and north of the Mayos, was a threat even to these values.

In the recent period we find consistent economic pressures actually becoming disintegrative to the economic autonomy of primary segments, whereas earlier effects of haciendas and mines were without such great consistency and operated largely on Mayos through Mayo choice. After 1890, the breakup of some of the communal lands and, after 1936, controls on planting crops through economic sanctions applied by the national ejido bank, are examples of the economic pressures of later periods.

Mayo economic organization also has been characterized by adaptive changes, however, such as steadily increasing tolerance of purchased goods, an adjustment to private ownership of lands to some extent, and an increasing tolerance of wage labor dating from fairly early times. On the whole, the Mayo economic system is still characterized by a household production unit, a positive value for primary resources, and an internal fiesta economy involving primary local segments rather than a national economy; and its adaptive responses are now occurring as primarily forced through directed change from national programs.

It must be noted, however, that an almost frozen wage scale, not emanating from the tribal social organization of the Mayo in any way, but imposed from the dominant society, does much to discourage adaptation to a cash market economy. For example, housing materials and the like must come from primary resources, such as stands of communally owned forest, for lack of cash income perhaps as much as from force of ancient custom.

5. MAYO INTEGRATION TODAY: TRIBE, CHIEFDOM, OR STATE SEGMENT?

RECONSIDERATION OF INITIAL HYPOTHESIS

The initial hypothesis suggested that Mayo society was characterized by a tribal integration, which in Service's (1962: 110-42) terms requires the presence of pan-tribal institutions, the economic autonomy of primary segments, and mechanical solidarity among tribal segments. Service further suggests a subcategory of tribe characterized by composite or cognatic organization, with bilateral kinship and loosely structured residence groups. In addition he suggests a number of other features usually found in connection with tribal level of organization, including sporadic warfare involving small numbers of individuals at any one time, but rather continual in nature and characterized by terroristic and supernatural methods as well as practical ones, and most external polity restricted to military action.

Most central in Service's scheme is the characteristic form of the residence unit. The basic residential units are like one another, largely autonomous, and largely self-sufficient economically. Also, in harmony with this mechanical kind of structure, and being large, they are politically fragile and tend to divide into pieces without the all-important mechanism of pan-tribal sodalities.

They share with the less complex band level of organization the characteristics of being familistic, egalitarian, in lacking separated bodies of political control and true full-time economic or religious specialization.

As we summarize the findings and compare them with Service's ideal type, it will be expected that Mayo society today varies somewhat importantly from a simple tribal organization. That does not invalidate the classification device nor does it render the Mayo data useless for a study of cultural evolution. On the contrary, the Mayo data may illuminate some of the processes involved in the change of type of other levels of sociocultural integration, particularly as related to contact changes, or what Service (1962) calls superorganic environment.

Mayo residence units are formed basically from households consisting of smaller kin units drawn from a large bilateral kin unit, on the basis of economic convenience. Households are grouped into rancherías, or clusters of households whose members do not intermarry. Both household and ranchería are exogamous. Within pueblos, or towns, there are analogous divisions known as barrios. Pueblos considered Mayo are frequently characterized by churches and often have resident within them persons in important ceremonial roles. The pueblo which has a church center, and the surrounding rancherías affiliated with it, form an organically integrated unit — households being connected with the church center in a variety of hierarchical and complementary patterns expressed mostly through ritual activities. In times of peace the integration of one pueblo-church center with another is a mechanical type of integration from the point of view of social organization. As we have pointed out, however, the cultural, as against social, organization of pueblo-to-pueblo integration is organic, in that each organization has a distinctive supernatural meaning and function not fully duplicated by any other pueblo.

Nevertheless, the basic form of Mayo intercommunity social integration, which is the criterion of classification of evolutionary development, is in peacetime a mechanical relationship and excludes non-Mayo communities.

Going further into the characteristics which confirm the essential tribal nature of Mayo organization, we can confirm the character and large number of pan-tribal sodalities in which so much time and cultural energy is invested. Men, women, and children participate in these sodalities. Almost every single Mayo individual participates in one or more within a period of no less than a decade of his life. In general, Mayo social organization has far over a hundred sociocentric Mayo statuses, most of which are in use in sodalities connected with the church-pueblo cult organization, whereas the egocentric statuses are fewer in number, not as well known by individuals, and far less often used throughout the community and large social circles than within the household.

Examples of sociocentric statuses are terms for

church and pueblo officials, sodality heads, and a proliferation of ranked statuses within each sodality. To identify an individual as parisero, for example, is to narrow him to one of some hundred and twenty men in a given church community; or as Pilato, is to narrow him to one of four or five; or to identify him as Pilato Segundo is to narrow to one individual known by the entire community and even by members of other communities.

By contrast, an egocentric, or kinship term relates the individual not to the community, but to an individual, or group of related individuals. Many Mayo in-law terms relate the affine to the child which connects the person to a kin group, thus referring indirectly to as many as three or four related persons. Nevertheless these kin terms relate to the family, and should be said to be, perhaps, "family-centric," and thus more narrow in group reference than the sodality status terms which refer to community roles. The pattern in which the old kinship system has been forgotten by most people, narrowing use of the Mayo terms to the nuclear family, shows that it has limited everyday use outside the nuclear family and the household. Even relatives are sometimes identified by their kin through sociocentric statuses, particularly by church or military sodality. The dead kin as well as the living are identified by use of sodality status.

The pueblo-church unit consisting, in the case of Bánari for example, of independent small farmers in five villages, was basically autonomous economically in the period in which the present organization crystalized. This was previous to 1890. However some regional specialization of Mayo communities occurs, and trade with money as a medium of exchange between Mayos is a deeply established pattern. The changing economy today is modifying that economic autonomy in ways that will be discussed.

Politically the pueblo is also autonomous. As we have demonstrated in regard to ceremonial exchange patterns, officials of equal status work together in councils where a pattern of mutual deference and unanimity is expected. In warfare, some hierarchical intervillage relationships have emerged in Mayo history, particularly in the second half of the 19th century, but systematic killing and deportation of leadership crippled the full unfolding of this process. The external polity of Mayo tribal organization with other Indian groups has been largely restricted to military conflict and, later, alliance for warfare; thus it has largely been related to offense-defense requirements.

Mayos have also, however, accepted refugee groups from the areas overrun by non-Mayos, and have themselves at different periods of their history formed refugee colonies among other communities of Cahitan peoples, as well as in Mexican and North American cities. The extent to which the latter processes have involved the interaction of formal pueblo organizations is probably small, however, since those organizations may well have been seriously undermined at any time when such complete flight was called for.

The integration of the pan-tribal sodalities with the religious life of the Mayos, and particularly with the church organization, makes the study of Mayo integration pivot on an understanding of the activities of ceremonial exchange between communities, as well as on the relationship of the curers and other more free-roving ceremonial specialists to this organization. The preceding chapters summarize what is felt to be the heart of this integration for Mayos. Some cross-Cahitan integration on the basis of both church-based and household-based ceremonial exchange and curer-clientele networks exists, but the intensity of internal Mayo River integration justifies an assumption of tribal limitations, combined with the self-identification of Mayos as a distinct people from Yaquis and Tehuecos, for example, and the existence of present and historical geographic boundaries recognized both by Mayos and neighboring groups.

Continual sporadic border warfare, a characteristic of many tribal level societies, seems to have ended with the mission period of Mayo history, inhibited by Spanish control rather than outgrown in a sense, but apparently never to recur in exactly the same form. After the mission period pan-tribal alliances appear, indicating a developing sophistication in intertribal polity. Nevertheless, the divisible character of Mayo tribal organization continued to be manifest up to the present time in factionalism and internal divisions of serious intensity both in the presence and absence of open conflict.

That supernatural means of terrorization connected with warfare probably existed prior to mission times is evidenced from the shamanistic powers associated with officers of the military societies. Today the war captain or bow chief has the authority to punish witches, and presumably is therefore able to recognize one. The taking of trophy body parts of valiant enemies, an earlier Cahitan trait, was apparently rare in more recent Mayo warfare, though it is reported as late as 1910.

TRAITS LEADING TO A MORE COMPLEX
LEVEL OF ORGANIZATION

Though Mayo organization has the diagnostic elements of the tribal level of integration and shares with the band level a familistic and egalitarian character, it borders on a more complex level of organization in some respects. Economic and religious specialization is relatively complex, but with the exception of one or two roles there are no full-time specialists.

Basic elements of the organization, on the other hand, which appear to lead toward a more advanced type of organization, specifically to what Service calls a chiefdom, for example, are fixed sacred boundaries. Some of these have dated markers (1775) which would tend to confirm that they were placed there during the Autonomous Period, and moreover following some of the Spanish attempts to break up Mayo land-holding patterns in 1771. However, the trend toward fixing boundaries was well under way in the end of the prehispanic period during the conflict of the Mayos with the Yaquis and the Fuerte River peoples, especially Tehuecos.

The combination of substantial population density and a tripartite physical ecology which would have permitted a chiefdom level organization may be documented early in Mayo history. Three physical zones were available with sandy coastline, giving access to fish and salt deposits, a fertile irrigable soil in the central river region, and cactus and leguminous forest fading into harder mesquite forest to the east and south. Some economic specialization of villages is indicated by informants as well as in historical sources. The occupational status terms, *birome* (fisherman), *'etléro* (farmer), and *'amuléro* (hunter), indicate differentiation of skills. Some people definitely do not fish, such as high ranking lifetime officials of the church and military societies. Others do all three types of activities but usually consider themselves to be predominantly involved in one occupation. The corn-raising farmer, who controls the high prestige food of traditional Mayo life, has the highest-ranking occupation. Fishing is the lowest-ranking. The people of Bánari consider themselves primarily a corn-growing people.

Mayo society is ideally egalitarian and imposes harsh sanctions such as witchcraft accusations and gossip on those who excel in any way beyond accepted bounds of economic or any other kind of equality. It has relatively few statuses elevated above that of the common man, and all are available to him. The life of an ordinary Mayo is said to be one of work and suffering. Any surplus that he may temporarily accumulate is expected to be shared with his less fortunate kin and compadres. Selfishness is a terrible sin, while generosity is a great virtue. The fiesta distribution system is an egalitarian kind of economic structure, which maintains equal prosperity and equal poverty in its ideal operating condition.

Nevertheless, even in the fiesta context, we see the incipient emergence of unequal statuses. The *tekiame*, those who have pueblo and church offices, and the paskola and maso groups (ceremonial dancers) are distinguished at fiestas from others by eating at a separate table. They are presented with sacred foods called by a different name than other foods, though the same essential food in fact, being served in first order by the highest ranking fiesteros. The authority of such high statuses is reflected in terms of address, each being distinguished by respect terms used by all members of the society, the use of special insignia, special positions in processions and other rituals. Having served in the top offices of a pueblo or church structure attaches a special aura of power to an individual, even after his service is ended. Periodic pueblo-church rituals reverse all established authority, however, to lower ranking officials, as if to remind the highest authorities that their power is held only by approval of popular will, which expresses divine sanctions.

Shamans and some ceremonial dancers have supernatural powers which derive from direct supernatural visions, an inherent kind of inequality which endows them with superiority of some varieties over ordinary people. They are not fully exempt from the dangers inherent in the accumulation of resources and their distribution outside the fiesta system, but they seem committed to economic as well as spiritual rules apart from the rest of the society. There are said to be grave supernatural dangers inherent in the kind of power those individuals have, so they must know how to use it. By becoming involved with a church organization, or by gaining support of its officials, they may add social power to their spheres of influence founded upon supernatural sanctions, clientele organizations, and charisma.

Fundamentally, however, other Mayo leadership is also largely individualistic, charismatic, and nonhereditary. And this is a tribal characteristic. Dream, vision, or battle experience is important in a number of high statuses in military society as well as for curers and some dancers, but usually it has to be ritually validated. Statuses such as maestro and sacristan require above all else the possession of appropriate knowledge and experience, leadership qualities, and commitment to the service of the supernaturals and to the pueblo. These roles are surrounded with sacred sanctions, as are the roles of the governors. They require a different and more subtle, but definite supernatural, validation from that of curer, for example.

The popular mandate is important for all leadership, and there are mechanisms for its concrete expression — far smoother in the case of church and pueblo governors, to be sure, where the Spanish system fused with native tribal democracy to provide a council in which the pueblo may express vocal approval of nominations by the appropriate officials. Consultation with a wide cross-section of the pueblo before making nominations is a safeguard to assure the proper choice. The rise of the heads of the Mayo church who have nominative power over governors is a less explicitly controlled process, though at first they are said to be chosen by the members of their respective sodalities, after long service and proof of leadership qualities. In fact, typically, the top leadership of these organizations tends to become a group of lifetime positions. Thus vast amounts of ritual and political knowledge and experience accumulate in the performance of these roles through their time- consuming character and centrality to community and intercommunity organization. They would appear to be the likely loci for the development of chief-like functions, especially in view of the fact that the church has a cash treasury and the church cults are the reason for the existence in a symbolic sense of the fiesta distribution system.

Two processes militate against the entrenchment of power in the office of the head maestro, or head sacristan, however. One is the balance of power in the council. The elders have a veto power over the nominations of the maestro, and he must consult with them before making nominations. Furthermore, though the Mayo church governors are appointed by the maestro and are under his authority in a real sense, the funds of the church are under lock and key to one of the governors, who must also use his own judgment in deciding when and how to disperse them. In the fiesta authority, the fiesteros are likewise independent in their spending activities as contrasted to their ritual activities, in which they are under command of the maestro and his head assistant. The maestro directly controls little or none of the economic wealth involved in the church and fiesta organization, though he ranks higher in authority and power than those who do — and that is, of course, interesting from an evolutionary point of view.

A second brake on the developing of a concentration of power in the role of head maestro or sacristan is the ritual opposition each spring in which the Parisero sodality temporarily commands the church organization. During this season, as shown in Figure 2, the church sodalities and officials, the men, women, and children of the pueblo, called by the names the Three Kings and the Three Marías, are temporarily taken into custody by the Lenten sodality. Though their seasonal dominance is temporary and incomplete, the Pariseros do function to balance power between leadership roles. The identification of the head maestro and church with the Child King and the Holy Trinity in Bánari, for example, confirms the importance of the government he represents and the supernatural sanction of his office. It is the incipient, but not fully formed, role of a priest-king. The pueblo organization is still too small and there are too many economic, demographic, and political reasons why that direction will not likely be taken in the future of Mayo integration.

MAYOS AS MEXICANS: A TRIBE WITHIN A STATE

The Mayo pueblo-church organization resembles in some respects a small theocratic city-state, though the religious hierarchy is not hereditary, nor is any part strictly so. Much of the present nature of these units developed or was much intensified in the mission and autonomous periods. In the pueblo and church, government is said to rise from popular will, and pueblo-wide councils are said to represent all the people. Mayo standards of lawful behavior generally prevail in the long run among Mayos in Mayo communities, and are voiced through the council and less explicit forms of public sanctions.

Mayo organization, then, looks like a curious conglomeration of traits of slightly varying versions of pan-tribal organization adapted for intertribal warfare in the prehispanic period, for mission community organization later, afterward for independent survival among intruding mining and hacienda colonies, and finally in the contexts of civil war and enclavement in a national state. The same transmutable but essentially unchanged set of church-military sodalities persisted and served in the process of survival.

It would appear at first that the organization is today "frozen" in an advanced level of tribal development confirmed in its present form largely during the Autonomous Period. But closer inquiry shows that a continuing series of developmental changes is going on today, though the growth of branches of leadership is consistently pruned through the intercultural ecology of enclavement in a state.

One of the current developmental processes, for example, is pueblo fission and development of new church centers, which has gone on in recent decades. Factionalism produces the fissions, and nativism heals the wounds. The larger number of church-pueblo cults provides adequate possibilities for an expanding Mayo population to participate in self-government. Rites of intensification and some rites of passage have been instituted in the new centers and elaborated. At least two nativistic movements have functioned to integrate household and church units into new nets of ceremonial exchange which may never before have been more closely knit, at least since the close of the Autonomous Period. This period was also characterized by intense nativism for Mayos.

Mayo ethnic identification is still intense (N. R. Crumrine 1964), and the mechanisms by which it is maintained are being extended into new areas through this mushrooming of ceremonial activity and the building of new churches. In the last twenty years the population of the Mayo River area has at least doubled. This, combined with the increasing rigidity of land boundaries, and the transformation through commercial exploitation of all three of the ecological zones traditionally associated with Mayo social organizational forms, may augur much more fundamental adaptations.

The members of Mayo society seem to be making desperate efforts to find successful organizational solutions to preserve their way of life and the most essential elements of their system of meaning for the world in the face of total ecological transformations more drastic than those which faced their ancestors some three and a half centuries ago. At that time a drastic population reduction in the functioning Mayo centers resulted rather suddenly in changing what may have been to that time a more closely kin-based organization into a kind of composite system in which essentially non-hereditary sodalities carried some of the compressed burden of symbolic knowledge and the obligation for its transmission. This knowledge had to that point been developed in a much larger society and must have been passed on in a very differently structured enculturation system. An enormous cultural loss must have occurred. Yet the survival of so much of the symbolism and social structure of prehispanic times in the face of the population reduction requires explanation.

Today the proportion of enculturation units to population size is quite the opposite. Considerable numbers of Mayos migrate to the edges of Sonoran Mexican cities, and almost everyone is reached as a result of the greater availability of schools, medical facilities through the ejidos, and a variety of media of learning such as books, newspapers, and cinema. Radio is particularly important, as the rural population is reached in almost every village in this way. Yet it is again astounding the degree to which new information from all sources is fitted into Mayo ethnic identity and how little it influences the hard core of social interaction patterns.

Though the means of production have undergone considerable change over that system which brought the present social organization into existence, and a market economy exists in the area in connection with the national economy, Mayos still tend to distribute the greater part of their surplus income in the Mayo fiesta distribution system. Through this integration of social, religious, and economic systems they maintain a distinctive society with its own processes of development enclaved within the Mexican national state.

The participation of Mayos in the voting and governmental structures, as well as in the military, of the Mexican national state, is limited. It is restricted by the part they play in the national economy and by the limited educational and social organizational links between them and the dominant society. Participation as Mexicans is also affected by the intensity of Mayo ethnic identity and the well-developed and apparently satisfying social organization by which Mayo identity is enhanced.

CONCLUSIONS

Mayo organization may be characterized as a modified tribal organization which has not changed type even though many of the elements of physical and superorganic environment in terms of which it originated have changed greatly. Most notably it is today enclaved in a national state which through the ejido system has a profound effect on its economic organization. The adaptive advantages of composite tribal organization for Mayos were in an early stage related to three factors: (1) Its usefulness in defensive warfare, possibly occasional offensive warfare, against tribes of comparable size (30,000) and of small chiefdoms of one or two thousand people. The boundary lines set up during the Autonomous Period suggest the Mayos may have been gaining land at the expense of the groups to the South, whereas they were at a bitter standstill with the Yaquis. (2) The effectiveness of sodality based organization to cope with enculturation and group integration in the face of floods and epidemics which periodically came into the area as a result of the river and ocean port location of the Mayo population, even aboriginally. (3) The advantages of having economic production units which were not strictly kin based but loosely structured, bilateral residence units which could adapt to changing land boundaries and even to a non-farm production system. This feature continued to be specially adaptive even as Mayos were brought into a new economy.

This underlying structure of pan-tribal sodalities continued during the mission period, a period of peace, based upon ceremonial exchange systems in which old sodality groups were integrated by priests through church rituals. At this time the Mayo economy was considerably enriched, but the social and economic adaptation pattern was basically the same as before. After the mission period and the withdrawal of the missionaries, the tribal organization proved useful again as a defense organization against isolated and fairly unorganized mestizo and Spanish colonists. It permitted a surprisingly effective defense against what were then in effect small chiefdom level mestizo organizations, and even with an incipient national state. The key to the fact that the Mayo organization, though still essentially tribal, was effective in holding out against an incipient national state

may well be that the Mayo adaptation to a specific total environment was more effective than the mestizo adaptation, until at least 1890. It may be understood in terms of the law of cultural dominance (Kaplan 1960: 75).

The Mayo organization dominated a specific environment primarily, though not solely, in terms of primary resources. The mestizo organization, which has become dominant over it, relates to a larger environment; a primarily regional economy gives way to a national, even a world economy. At the same time the holdout of a tribal organization for so long a time against a frontier state can be explained also in terms of the law of cultural dominance. Pan-tribal sodalities provided effective defense and intercommunity communication combined with a fiesta distribution system which spread the surplus products of the entire valley to all pueblos, and an elastic production unit adaptable to population and residence changes. In the Autonomous Period this system was more general than the hacienda system, whose major object was to support one family in a grand style at the expense of hundreds of peons.

The tribal organization, periodically regenerated through recent periods, has functioned chiefly to maintain Mayo identity through enculturation. It has suffered increasing economic and demographic frustration as mestizo culture, supported by the national economy, has hemmed it in.

It seems possible that the "potentiality of backwardness" (Service 1960: 97-103) could apply to the Mayo organization, that it could form the basis for development of local governments within a state system. It seems possible it might become highly democratic in form without ever having passed through a fully characteristic chiefdom level of organization. But this does not seem to be happening. Much of the future development of Mayo social organization depends on activities of the different officials and agencies in the dominant society both on the local and national levels, the types of directed change which its various authorities are applying, and the ways in which Mayo leadership is allowed to participate in the incorporation of Mayo society into the dominant society.

GLOSSARY

The following words are Mayo or Spanish loan words (in which case Spanish spelling may be used; e.g. *gracia* instead of *grasia*). Pronunciation of Mayo vowels is generally similar to those of Spanish, for practical purposes, as are consonants. In Mayo words the symbol "c" has been used for "č". The accent falls on the first syllable of a Mayo word unless otherwise noted by written accent.

ʔ*abari* — corn roasted whole on the cob.

ʔ*alawasin* — "sheriff"; lowest ranking member of the fiesteros.

ʔ*alperes* — flagbearer; second-ranking member of the fiesteros.

ʔ*alwasil* — "sheriff"; an officer in the matachini society, ranking below the head monarca.

ʔ*amulero* — hunter.

ʔ*ápateak* — owner, landlord; literally, "he owns (it)"; said of a man who has had a vision of a saint and makes an image of the saint which can then be used in ceremonies.

ʔ*asóaka* — said of a woman having many children.

barrio — (Spanish), a district of a pueblo or city; for Mayos, an exogamous unit.

birome — fisherman.

ejido — (Spanish), a communal land-holding unit which may either be divided into separate land assignments or farmed communally by the members of the association to whom the land is assigned by federal authority. It includes common village forest as well as cultivated fields.

ʔ*Espiritu Santu* — Holy Spirit. In Arócosi, the patron saint, ʔEspiritu Santu, is known as ʔItom ʔAye, Our Mother.

ʔ*etlero* — farmer.

goʔim — coyotes, members of a division of the Mayo military society.

gracia — (Spanish), the grace, from a vision or manifestation of God, to cure illness, believed to be possessed by Mayo native herb-doctors.

hemyori — literally "to rest," also applied to the ritual pause or recess in a procession at the altar of a household before proceeding to the fiesta-giving household or church.

hisobare — loin or tender meat roasted on skewers over an open flame.

hitolio — herbal doctor, believed to possess supernatural power to diagnose causes of illness and cure witchcraft caused diseases.

ʔ*Itom ʔAcai* — any form of Our Father, Jesus, Christ Child, Christ Crucified; the Father God (ʔItom ʔAcai, ʔOʔola). Sans ʔIsidro, the churchyard cemetery cross and other crosses or any other manifestation of male divinity.

ʔ*Itom ʔAcai, ʔUsi* — Our Father Son, Jesus.

ʔ*Itom ʔAye* — any form of Our Mother, any of the Three Marys, the Holy Mother, Mary Magdalene, Mary Dolorosa, Santa Teresa, the earth, the church, some crosses, or any manifestation of female divinity.

kowinohim — pork tamales, strips of lean pork covered with moistened corn meal and steamed in corn husks.

kurus yoʔowe — "great cross." a generic term applied to the pueblo boundary cross, the churchyard cross, the dance ramada cross, and several other crosses central to Mayo ceremonial life and treated as saints.

lisénsia — permission; lisénsia for intercommunity exchange of church groups, and even individual visits in some cases, must pass through the proper pueblo and church councils and sodality heads.

maestro moʔoro — assistant to the maestro, a very active role in which guidance of the fiesteros through rituals is the chief task. The ritual insignia of this role is a thin drum, often beaten while leading the fiesteros.

maestro yoʔowe — head lay minister of a Mayo church, who reads prayers, plays an important part not only in the performance of home and church ritual but also in all important religious and community decisions apart from and through the council.

maestro — lay minister. Mayo church maestros form a sodality with internal rankings and organization.

mala — (man speaking) daughter.

manda — ritual promise made by a family or individual to a saint to give a fiesta for the saint in the event that a severe sickness is cured or personal crisis passes safely.

[49]

maso — deer, or deer dancer; ritual dance specialist who performs at fiestas and is associated with a body of myth and sacred literature.

masobaki — deer stew.

matachin — a member of a dance society closely associated with the church organization, whose mature male members dance at almost every major household and church event outside the Lenten season, and into which the adolescent boys and girls of the downriver Mayo area are initiated during the fiestas of Trinity and Epiphany Sundays.

monarca — dance leader of the matachin society.

mo²oro — helper assistant, as maestro mo²oro, assistant maestro.

municipio — (Spanish), administrative unit in the political system of Mexico similar to a county in respect to geographical size, but administered through a non-local, centralized, essentially one-party system through local appointees.

nakúlia — literally exchange or change; specifically a "rosary," or item used ritually to cement solidarity within a Mayo sodality, or between incoming and outgoing members.

nuhmeame — (man speaking), sons-in-law, literally warriors.

panim nakúliam — bread rosaries, large strings of bread, oranges, limes, and squashes used in a ritual to guard against ill will which might otherwise divide the solidarity of the groups of fiestero sodalities performing in the Santisima Tiniran-Espiritu Santu exchange.

parinam — highest ranking fiesteros.

pariseros — men's Lenten sodality acting out the part of the army pursuing, capturing, and crucifying Jesus for a period of seven weeks between Ash Wednesday and Easter. Parisero officers remain important until May 3, and may be assigned community tasks at any time in the year.

paskola — a costumed ritual dance specialist, performing animal dances to the flute and drum or harp and violins, at house and pueblo fiestas, and whose activities are associated with a body of sacred literature and mythology.

paskome — fiesteros, or those who give the fiesta. Being a fiestero implies having made a manda to a saint and having been cured. The duties of the fiestero imply ceremonial labor, food-giving.

Pilato — Pilate, top-ranking officers of the parisero sodality, felt by Mayos to be wise in ritual knowledge.

rancheria — (Spanish), group of households, usually removed in geographical distance from other settlements. For Mayos the unit is exogamous.

sakobari — watermelon.

San Juan Bautista — Saint John the Baptist.

San Rafael — Saint Raphael, patron of Tosalipaku, called ²Itom²Aye, or Our Mother by Mayos in the villages downriver.

Santa Kurus — Holy Cross. A white flowered cross known to many Mayos as ²Itom²Acai; however, also known by some as ²Itom ²Aye, patron of Homecarit.

Santisima Tiniraŋ — Holy Trinity. Patron saint of Bánari, an image of three young men on whose chests are a lamb, an eye within a triangle, and a dove, surrounded by cherubim and seraphim in clouds. The Santisima Tiniran image of a nearby village, Huícori, where it is also patron, differs considerably.

tekiame — those who have pueblo and church offices validated by the people through council approval.

totoribaki — chicken stew.

wakabaki — beef stew, a fiesta food.

wikicim — (*wikit*, sing.) birds, members of a segment of the Mayo military society.

REFERENCES

ACOSTA, ROBERTO
  1949 *Apuntes Historicos Sonorenses, La Conquista Temporal y Espiritual del Yaqui y del Mayo*. Imprinta Aldina, Mexico, D. F.

BARNES, J. A.
  1962 African Models in the New Guinea Highlands. *Man* 62: 5-9.

BEALS, RALPH
  1932 Comparative Ethnography of Northern Mexico before 1750. *Ibero-Americana* 2: 94-225.

  1943 The Aboriginal Culture of the Cahita Indians. *Ibero-Americana* 19.

  1945 The Contemporary Culture of the Cahita Indians. *Bureau of American Ethnology, Bulletin* 142. Washington.

BENNETT, WENDELL C., AND ROBERT M. ZINGG
  1935 *The Tarahumara, An Indian Tribe of Northern Mexico*. University of Chicago Press, Chicago.

BOHANNAN, LAURA, AND PAUL BOHANNAN
  1953 The Tiv of Central Nigeria. *Ethnographic Survey of Africa: Western Africa*, Part VIII. International African Institute, London.

BOHANNAN, PAUL
  1958 Extra-processual Events in Tiv Political Institutions. *American Anthropologist* 60: 1-12.

BUNZEL, RUTH
  1952 Chichicastenango: A Guatemalan Village. *Publications of the American Ethnological Society* XXII.

CRUMRINE, N. ROSS
  1964 The House Cross of the Mayo Indians of Sonora, Mexico. *Anthropological Papers of the University of Arizona*, No. 8. University of Arizona Press, Tucson.

DABDOUB, CLAUDIO
  Historia de El Valle del Yaqui. Liberia de Manuel Porrua, S. A. Mexico.

ERASMUS, CHARLES J.
  1952 The Leader vs. Tradition: A Case Study. *American Anthropologist* 54: 168-78.

  1961 *Man Takes Control, Cultural Development and American Aid*. University of Minnesota Press. Minneapolis.

ESTADO DE SONORA
  1957 Proyecto de Programa de Gobierno del Estado de Sonora. *Tabasco*, 275. Impressiones Modernas, S. A.

EVANS-PRITCHARD, E. E.
  1940 *The Nuer, A Description of the Modes of Livelihood and Political Institutions of a Nilotic People*. Clarendon Press. Oxford.

FORTES, MEYER
  1936 Ritual Festivals and Social Cohesion in the Hinterland of the Gold Coast. *American Anthropologist* 38: 590-604.

GILL, MARIO
  1957 *La Conquista del Valle del Fuerte*. Impresora Técnica Moderna, S. A. México 7, D. F.

HAMMOND, GEORGE P., AND AGAPITO REY (translators, editors)
  1928 *Obregon's History of 16th Century Explorations in Western America, Entitled Chronicle, Commentary, or Relation of the Ancient and Modern Discoveries in New Spain and New Mexico, Mexico, 1584*. Wetzel Publishing Company, Inc., Los Angeles.

KAPLAN, DAVID
  1960 The Law of Cultural Dominance. In *Evolution and Culture*, M. Sahlins and E. R. Service, editors. University of Michigan Press, Ann Arbor.

KENNEDY, JOHN G.
  1963 Tesquino Complex: The Role of Beer in Tarahumara Culture. *American Anthropologist* 65: 620-40.

LEACH, EDMUND R.
    1954 *Political Systems of Highland Burma*,
          London.

LEWIS, OSCAR
    1963 *Life in a Mexican Village: Tepoztlán
          Revisited*. University of Illinois Press,
          Urbana.

OBREGON, ALVARO
    1959 Ocho Mil Kilometros en Campaña.
          Fondo de Cultura Económica (Primera
          Ed. 1917). México 12, D. F.

PÉREZ DE RIBAS, P. ANDRÉS, S. J.
    1944 *Historia de Los Triunfos de Nuestra
          Santa Fe Entre Gentes Las Más Bár-
          baras y Fieras del Nuevo Orbe . . .
          México*. Editorial Layac.

REDFIELD, ROBERT, AND
          ALFONSO VILLA ROJAS
    1962 *Chan Kom, A Maya Village*. University
          of Chicago Press, Chicago.

SAHLINS, MARSHALL D.
    1961 The Segmentary Lineage: An Organi-
          zation of Predatory Expansion. *Amer-
          ican Anthropologist* 63: 322-45.

SAHLINS, MARSHALL D., AND
          ELMAN R. SERVICE (editors)
    1960 *Evolution and Culture*. University of
          Michigan Press, Ann Arbor.

SERVICE, ELMAN R.
    1960 The Law of Evolutionary Potential. In
          Evolution and Culture. Marshall D.
          Sahlins and Elman R. Service, editors,
          University of Michigan Press, Ann
          Arbor.

    1962 *Primitive Social Organization, An Evo-
          lutionary Perspective*. Random House,
          New York.

SIBLEY, WILLIS
    1960 The Maintenance of Unity and Distinc-
          tiveness by a Philippine Peasant Vil-
          lage. In *Men and Cultures*. Anthony F.
          C. Wallace, editor. University of Penn-
          sylvania Press, Philadelphia.

SPICER, EDWARD H.
    1940 *Pascua, A Yaqui Village in Arizona*.
          University of Chicago Press, Chicago.

    1943 Linguistic Aspects of Yaqui Accultura-
          tion. *American Anthropologist* 45:
          410-26.

    1945 El Problema Yaqui. *America Indigena*
          5: 273-86.

    1947a Yaqui Militarism. *Arizona Quarterly*
          3: 40-8.

    1947b Yaqui Villages Past and Present. *The
          Kiva* 13: 1.

    1954a Potam, A Yaqui Village in Sonora.
          *American Anthropological Association
          Memoir* 77.

    1954b Spanish-Indian Acculturation in the
          Southwest. *American Anthropologist*
          56: 663-78.

    1961 Yaqui. In *Perspectives in American
          Indian Culture Change*. Edward H.
          Spicer, editor. University of Chicago
          Press, Chicago.

    1962 *Cycles of Conquest, The Impact of
          Spain, Mexico and the United States
          on the Indians of the Southwest,
          1533-1960*. University of Arizona
          Press, Tucson.

    1964 Apuntes Sobre El Tipo de Religion de
          Los Yuto-Aztecas Centrales. *Actas y
          Memorias*. XXXV Congresso Interna-
          cional de Americanistas. México.

SPICER, ROSAMOND B.
    1949 People on the Desert. In *The Desert
          People, a Study of the Papago Indians*,
          by Alice Joseph, Rosamond B. Spicer,
          and Jane Chesky. University of Chi-
          cago Press, Chicago.

STEPHEN, ALEXANDER M.
    1936 Hopi Journal of Alexander M.
          Stephen. Elsie Clews Parsons, editor.
          *Columbia University Contributions to
          Anthropology* 23.

STEVENSON, MATILDA COX
    1905 The Zuni Indians. *23rd Annual Report
          of the Bureau of American Ethnology*,
          Washington.

STEWARD, JULIAN H.
    1955 *Theory of Culture Change*. University
          of Illinois Press, Urbana.

TRONCOSO, FRANCISCO P.
    1905 *Las Guerras con las Tribus Yaqui y
          Mayo del Estado de Sonora, México*.

UNDERHILL, RUTH MURRAY
    1939 Social Organization of the Papago In-
          dians. *Columbia University Contribu-
          tions to Anthropology* 30.

ANTHROPOLOGICAL PAPERS OF THE UNIVERSITY OF ARIZONA

1. **EXCAVATIONS AT NANTACK VILLAGE, POINT OF PINES, ARIZONA**
David A. Breternitz
The excavation of eleven semi-subterranean pithouses, including a Great Kiva, defines the Nantack Phase of the Black River Branch of the Mogollon Culture.
79 pp. $1.75

2. **YAQUI MYTHS & LEGENDS**   Ruth W. Giddings
Now in book format.   190 pp. $3.95

3. **MAROBAVI: A STUDY OF AN ASSIMILATED GROUP IN NORTHERN SONORA**   Roger C. Owen
The lag between cultural and social assimilation in the process of acculturation is revealed in this study of a rural *mestizo* community in northeast Sonora.
70 pp. $1.50

4. **A SURVEY OF INDIAN ASSIMILATION IN EASTERN SONORA**   Thomas Hinton
Three aboriginal groups — Opata, Jova, and Pima — are traced on their way to complete physical and cultural absorption into surrounding Mexican populations.
32 pp. $1.50

5. **THE PHONOLOGY OF ARIZONA YAQUI**   Lynn S. Crumrine
Literal and free translations of conversational responses flesh out this analysis — including stress, tone, and pause — of the phonemics of an Arizona dialect of Yaqui.
43 pp. $2.00

6. **THE MARICOPAS: AN IDENTIFICATION FROM DOCUMENTARY SOURCES**   Paul Ezell
Ethnographic sleuthing identifies Indian occupants of the Gila-Colorado area from clues found in the reports of travelers from Onate (1604–1605) to the 49ers.
29 pp. $2.25

7. **THE SAN CARLOS INDIAN CATTLE INDUSTRY**   Harry Getty
Examination of a case of directed culture change containing a detailed historical account of the introduction and development of the cattle business on the San Carlos Apache reservation.   87 pp. $3.25

8. **THE HOUSE CROSS OF THE MAYO INDIANS OF SONORA, MEXICO**   Ross Crumrine
The problem of Mayo ethnic identity analyzed in terms of the mechanisms by which individuals recognize members of their own or another social group — in this case the house cross and its integration with other symbols.
57 pp. $3.00

9. **SALVAGE ARCHAEOLOGY IN PAINTED ROCK RESERVOIR, WESTERN ARIZONA**   William W. Wasley & Alfred E. Johnson
The first major report since *Excavations at Snaketown* reconstructs the Hohokam culture in an examination of other excavation sites, artifacts, and petroglyphs in the Gila Bend area of Arizona. Profusely illustrated.
123 pp. $5.00

10. **AN APPRAISAL OF TREE-RING DATED POTTERY IN THE SOUTHWEST**   David A. Breternitz
The interpretation of more than 5700 dated tree-ring specimens from some 340 archaeological sites in the American Southwest is the basis for "dating" the pottery types found in association. Time involved spans the period from the introduction of fired ceramics to about A.D. 1550.   128 pp. $5.00

11. **THE ALBUQUERQUE NAVAJOS**   William H. Hodge
Clears up hitherto unexplored questions about urban Indians. Comparison of the case histories of the 275 adult Navajos living in Albuquerque during the years 1959–61 reveals how and why some Indians adjust while others do not.   96 pp. $4.00

12. **PAPAGO INDIANS AT WORK**   Jack O. Waddell
Notable new discoveries concerning American Indian acculturation. Intensive analysis of the adaptive experiences of five Papago laborers working in four different occupational environments points up new social roles and modified behavior patterns.   160 pp. $5.00

13. **CULTURE CHANGE & SHIFTING POPULATIONS IN CENTRAL NORTHERN MEXICO**   William B. Griffen
A well-organized historical investigation of culture contact between raiding aboriginal Indian groups and Spanish colonists in central northern Mexico. Significant insights concerning conflicting concepts of ownership and property.   192 pp. $6.00

14. **CEREMONIAL EXCHANGE AS A MECHANISM IN TRIBAL INTEGRATION AMONG THE MAYOS OF NORTHWEST MEXICO**   Lynne S. Crumrine
The first ethnographic account of a Mayo community of the traditional type, and the only community study undertaken from the point of view of the inter-relationships of the cultural elements. Gives a new and broader understanding of the nature of the community type that generally developed among Middle American Indians following Spanish contact.   64 pp. $4.00

THE UNIVERSITY OF ARIZONA PRESS, Box 3398, College Station, Tucson, Arizona 85700